To *A Nação*, with Love:

The Politics of Language through Angolan Poetry

Robert Simon

To *A Nação*, with Love:

The Politics of Language through Angolan Poetry

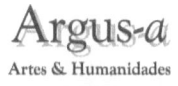
Artes & Humanidades

Argus-*a*
Artes y Humanidades / Arts and Humanities
Buenos Aires - Los Ángeles
2017

To *A Nação*, with Love: The Politics of Language through Angolan Poetry

ISBN 978-1-944508-09-8

Diseño de tapa: Argus-*a*

On the cover, photo of the 4th of April bridge over the Catumbela river, Lobito, Republic of Angola

Author: Augusto Pombo
Owner: INEA – Instituto de Estradas de Angola (Angolan Roads Authority)
Designer: ARMANDO RITO ENGENHARIA, SA
Contractor: JV MOTA-ENGIL / SOARES DA COSTA
Supervision: ISQ

Authorized by INEA and the photographer.

© 2017 Robert Simon

All rights reserved. This book or any portion thereof may not be reproduced or used in any manner whatsoever without the express written permission of the publisher except for the use of brief quotations in a book review or scholarly journal.

Editorial Argus-*a*
16944 Colchester Way,
Hacienda Heights, California 91745
U.S.A.

Calle 77 No. 1976 – Dto. C
1650 San Martín – Buenos Aires
ARGENTINA
argus.a.org@gmail.com

For Sophia and Helena, where my heart belongs;

for those who will find inspiration within these pages;

and for all those who have believed in something greater;

agradeço-vos enormemente...

Acknowledgements

I would like to acknowledge the following people and sources for their help and support in the creation of this book:

- The Sturgis Library at Kennesaw State University, and in particular, the Library's Interlibrary Loan Staff, for your talents at helping me find some pretty inaccessible texts;
- The Editors and Staff of Argus-*a*, for your faith in my work;
- Olaf Berward, the Chair of the Department of Foreign Languages at Kennesaw State University, who lent his support both in spirit and in action during the composition of this book;
- Fernando Arenas, for your counsel and wisdom, past, present, and future;
- Inocência Matta, for the inspiration your prose has given me;
- Ana Mafalda Leite, for offering a perspective on the Angolan literary experience so similar to my own;
- Luís Kandjimbo, for sharing your work so openly with me and with the world; and
- My family, friends, and colleagues who have stood by me all this time.

Thank you / Obrigado!

Table of Contents

Introduction: A Theoretical Framework   1

Chapter I: A Sociopolitical Background for Angola and Lusophone Africa   21

Chapter II: History and Poetry in Contemporary Angola   37

Chapter III: Phase I – the struggle for self and nation   73

Chapter IV: Phase II – the struggle for nation's self   127

Conclusions   163

Notes   173

Appendix   177

Works Cited   179

Introduction: *A Theoretical Framework*

It may be taken as an axiom that countries and nations rely on the authority invested in them in order that they may protect the populace and maintain social order. In most cases this implies that they grant themselves a certain power beyond that which would implicitly fall, and be kept, in the hands of the people. This may include, although are not limited to, the authority to exploit the use of military and / or police force in order that the governing body may impose its brand of control, moving even toward the incentivized and / or forced removal of peoples from one region to another. They also use their power to remove cultures (not necessarily peoples) from their national territories in order that a given regime's perceived authority may be nurtured without extraneous preoccupation.

It may also be taken as an axiom that the people must have a mode of expression which surpasses that of any particular government, in support of that body, in opposition to it, or independent of political concerns. This may take many forms, such as protest, art, music, mass media such as television or film, or (in many cases) a combination / combinations of these. Cultural expression within any given country or nation is the key to understanding its internal workings and the effects of these on the peoples living there. Literature, in many ways, can serve either to help to protect and support that power, or to criticize and (in this postmodern, or even post-postmodern, world) denaturalize it so as to remove the false objectivity with which it may become overreaching or even dangerous.

To complicate matters, the politics of language also play an essential role in determining who builds and keeps a power base in a region or country, and what the majority can do to survive, or even flourish, in that context. Again, this may give rise to a confluence between literature and language, in terms of the creation or criticism of cultural hegemonies and / or explicit power structures. When literary arts become limited to a specific language, particularly in a region in which the historical, political, or other actions of people using that language suppress (or at least imply a suppression of) specific groups, then the act of literary creation itself, insofar as it supports the institutional building of a nation where one did not before exist, may be open to criticism. Marginalized peoples may find their own voice; however, it will usually have to come from within the majority language in order that it may be heard. They may also find themselves spoken for by writers of that majority whose representations, both flattering and deceiving, drag them into a sort of undesirable-desired symbolic of a self-contradicting national identity.

Such is the situation in Angola. The builders of the current government saw the place of the literary as a way to foment a sense of nation, in large part through the use of a particular language, namely, that of the former colonizer which the new national leaders had adopted as their own. (Whether or not this language combines with other, "indigenous" languages or not will reveal various aspects of the process of appropriation). Poetry, in conjunction with (and at times even above) prose, with its condensed metaphorical significance and unconstrained fluidity and transformed into one of the central artistic genres in expressing two principle social and political trajectories, takes center stage in this unique process. Here the reader will observe two major periods in Angolan poetry in terms of language use and expressions of / reflections on notions of power.

The first will be the desire on the part of the soon-to-be new governing body to create a new nation during the war of independence. This nation's sociopolitical history would place it into a position whereby its forced linguistic simplification and subsequent evolution would serve the soon-to-be ruling party's discourse of Angolan national identity. The second poetic movement will counter this ideal, taking into account what this brave new world stands to lose in its quest for nationhood. In neither case does the altruistic love of nation become a simple decision of affirmation vs. negation. It is evident that writers in this first "phase" of poetic discourse in nation building express their adoration for their homeland through an exalted sense of oneness; in the second, writers employ techniques in order to criticize through a critical eye the idealism of the first.[1]

The reason for this book's creation has to do with the missing, yet vital, piece of the puzzle of attempting to create a relatively unified, Angolan identity, or *Angolanidade*. No matter how imagined it may seem, the Angolan MPLA-led government has invested time and resources into building an infrastructure in which the dominant language of the elite, Portuguese, has become that of the majority. The mode which this government has used did not surge forth from a position of isolation; rather, it feeds out from a longer and more nuanced process of linguistic dissemination and acculturation beginning centuries earlier.[2] As such, one would assume that studies of this very particular and uniquely visible phenomenon exist. Yet outside of a few short mentions of the language in the work of Chabal and Matta (and even then it is usually in the context of citing literature or of contextualizing Angola within the PALOP sphere), no work has of late come forth which seeks to theorize on what seems, at least on a superficial level, to have been the language's unexpectedly rapid spread *as a natively spoken language* (as opposed to one which takes on the aspects of a "lingua franca" for the region) from the country's urban areas of Luanda and Benguela into all but the most isolated regions of Angola's

borderlands, and even less so on how such a process finds its expression through poetry, despite the various critical frameworks designed around the former and then the latter, respectively.[3]

---

[1] This binary process sets the stage for revelations about the future expunging of the same diversity for which the first phase seemed to stand.

[2] I will focus a bit more on the complex issue of finding solid data, insofar as may be possible, on the percentage of native Angolan Portuguese speakers in the next chapter.

[3] It should first be noted that this study is not at all the first definitive study on Angolan poetry, nor on power relations in Angolan literatures. Several critics, such as Afolabi, Arenas, Basto, Birmingham, Leite, and Matta, among many others, have done so. Their work will appear cited throughout this book. Rather, it means to offer an alternative focus on those relations, and to propose an analysis of sociocultural expression through

The analysis presented in this book, then, finds itself in the position of being very unique in terms of its point(s) of focus, and for its breadth and depth within this / these. It endeavors to give the most objective view possible to the sociopolitical, critical, and artistic issues at hand by way of an illustration of contemporary perspectives on the interconnectivity between language, literature, and historical processes. Such a study hopes to invite discussion along the lines brought forth in pages to follow.

As such an evolution (perhaps the term "(r)evolution" would serve more aptly) of the literary as a reflection of the extra-literary evidently cannot exist in a vacuum. Thus, the study brings together first a more general outline of the macro-level processes of language use, change, adoption, dissemination, and immediate link with the social and political. It turns ever more toward the specific case at hand, that is, Angola of the pre- and post-independence periods, c. 1950-2002, the period in which the territory moved from its status as a Portuguese colony to that of independent country whose political discourse would express its place in the throes of its own unfolding as a supposedly unified, developing nation.

Before beginning the discussion summarized above, however, it is necessary to expound first on the reasons why literature, and particularly poetry, should be taken as such a vital means by which these topics may find a most appropriate exploration. In this way the absolute need for such a study will serve to evidence itself.

No literary critic, reader, or experienced political leader would doubt the importance of literature and poetry in the expression of individual, local, or national identity in any successful, or at least survived, country on earth. This holds true particularly for the relatively newer countries of Contemporary Africa. Insomuch as the pre-independence

---

linguistic (among other) considerations in poetry. Also, even though I will mention specifically a prose author in this study, as well as reference major theories surrounding prosaic work, this study's principle genre of focus will remain poetry.

period of most countries saw the growth of sentiments surrounding the ideal of nationhood, bolstered in the postcolonial African sociopolitical context through official and unofficial policy and practice, the praxis of such a notion could not have happened without first the complete support of the artistic apparatus, followed by the nuanced criticism of the political (many times at odds with stated, official goals for the nation) at and beyond the turn of the 20th Century.

Yet a problem emerges with respect to the analysis of texts in reference to their places of origin. There exists a tendency in the reading of literary works to approach them, essentially, in isolation from context, either in order to study thoroughly the unique literary techniques (the use of tropes, poetic device, etc.) or to find how the text's expression of a context corresponds best with a specific literary framework, taking into account the literary as a reflection of culture only as literary object rather than a work's reason to be. This literary trajectory has made itself apparent in recent years with the resurgence of what some have called the "surface reading" of a text, or the apparent adversity to the deeper, multifaceted reading of polysemy within a text.[4] Yet, this approximation may lead the informed reader down a dangerous path. As Ahluwalia has stated:

> [P]ost-colonial theory has often been characterised as being epistemologically indebted to both post-structuralism and postmodernism. Such a reading denigrates the authenticity of post-colonial theory and renders it subservient and theoretically vulnerable to charges levelled at post-structuralism and postmodernism. (138)

Although true that one may read and re-read the post-colonial text within a theoretically-oriented guise of the postmodern, a denatured approach would only impoverish an overall understanding of it. In this sense one must reincorporate the text into its context, that is, view a work

---

[4] For more information on this topic in contemporary literary criticism, one may consult Best and Marcus' work, cited at the end of this study.

of literature as an essential element of a culture's whole body. This body will be in constant evolution; its literature must epistemologically follow suit.

As an example of an attempt at reconciling the theoretical and the contextual within a critical framework is that of Ramazani when he states, on the one hand, that "[i]f one concept of modernist poetry is poetry that responds to modernity, then surely Post-colonial poets of Africa ... belong in a collection of essays on Modernist poetry," and on the other, that:

> Postcolonial poets have thus written out of the disjunctions and layerings of transgeographic experience, produced by migration, modernity and colonialism, even when they have been fiercely attached to the local soil. As such, they have created a poetry that is often a cacophony of discrepant idioms and genres, landscapes and images, gathered from local sites and from far-flung corners of the world. In its transnational reach, in its intercultural bearings, such poetry recalls the work of the Anglo-modernists, emergent during an earlier stage of globalisation. (219-20)

There is both a rejuvenating and disheartening aspect to this interpretation. It views poetry of Africa as quintessentially behind the times, while striving to defend it by triggering the terminology which highlights its uniqueness as a continent-wide phenomenon (another self-contradicting conclusion in need of further analysis).

Another aspect to consider is one of genre: most literary critics and critical readers of such texts have focused rather deeply on prose, perhaps as part of a general push in recent times toward the prizing of this form above that of poetry, a form more preferred traditionally among writers and students of literature. As such, while a substantial opus of critical studies exists on prose works from contemporary Africa, relatively few exist on poetry, and fewer still which focus on the societal causation of the variety of poetic engenderment which observed today. As an example of one such study, Gohar's comparative work on the verses

Langston Hughes and of the Sudanese poet Mohammed Al-Fayturi is informative thematically yet discusses the Sudanese experience and the African-American experience as somehow equally "African" (42). This perspective does have a place within the Pan-African view; yet, it tends toward generalization to the point of losing the individually regional, "national," intra- and inter-national, etc., losing again a level of specificity appropriate to the study of more locally-oriented concerns. In that, a study such as the one I propose here means to break away from a universalizing structure insofar as it may bind the reader to a false sense of African singularity in order to look more closely at the situation in Angola.

In any case, and returning to the topic of literary form selection for such a study, there is a need to analyze poetry as an equally meritorious vehicle for the transmission of the profound individual and collective experiences of societies (whether in isolation or as part of a larger regional movement) in a rapidly changing political context. This could be related to the idea that song has served to express feelings toward the social aspect of the self in various societies in Africa (Mirabeau 309).[5] Dali points out, for example, that poets such as Viriato da Cruz and Tomás Vieira da Cruz, rather than prose authors, utilize their verses to establish a link between the form and content of urban Angolan society in the pre-independence period of the 1950s (289-90). From the 1960s through independence, in fact, poetry had become the most visible and "commonplace" mode of literary expression in Lusophone Africa, and particularly Angola:

> Apart from the advantages of this literary mode, it has been by force of circumstance the most convenient: in many cases, the only outlet has been newspapers, small literary magazines and journals, where it would have been impossible to publish full-scale novels. (Hughes 18)

---

[5] It should be noted that Mirabeau's statement basis its logic on the principle of African unity, applying that universalized notion to a particular case in Cameroon. I will comment on this phenomenon in literary criticism in subsequent portions of this study.

Prose seems to catch up later on (and becomes the more studied of the two literary forms in recent times), with the study of film and its metaphoric imagery following closely behind.[6] In order to find a similarly expressive argument in favor of the study of poetry in a close vein with that of prose and film today, it is necessary to invoke the voice of Russell Hamilton, one of the founding intellectuals of Lusophone-African literary studies as it exists today, in his discussion of what he had considered "Euro-Mozambican" poets:

> [A] theory of a revolutionary literary aesthetic is not solely a matter of the intrinsic elements of a poem or body of literature; it is also a question of how a poem or story functions in relation to a number of societal and political factors. ... [these poets] ... tended to situate poetry in a prescribed social space. In the contemporary Western World poetry has been placed in such a restricted space as to become almost obsolete as a medium of communal cultural discourse ... the poetry of cultural revindication and social protest that emerged in colonial Luanda and Lourenço Marques [modern-day Maputo] was designed to awaken the social consciousness of a broad audience. ("Posturing," 163-64)

Hamilton's word, in a way, echo the call to action on the part of 1950s and 60s Luso-African poets. They serve in reminding the reader of the necessity for a balanced approach when measuring the current focus on prosaic and filmic arts with the evident applicability of the poetic in both lyrical / intimate and socially-pertinent terms. In this sense, it becomes not only recommended, but vital, to study poetry and its evolution as a vehicle for the expression of cultural evolution, particularly in emerging and uniquely placed nations (in linguistic, historical, and political terms) such as Angola.

---

[6] Sarah Maldoror's 1996 essay on filmic language and socio-political attitudes, as well as Paulette Hacker's study of the Mauritanian cinematographer Abderrahmane Sissako's *La vie sur terre*, serve as recent examples of such a focus.

Here, then, I will return to the topics of language, politics, and the poetic expression of these, with a brief discussion of the use of European languages in contemporary sub-Saharan Africa. It will briefly outline general issues of language politics and use from both a prescriptive and descriptive lens, emphasizing areas in which both a broken social contract with respect to certain examples from the so-called "Anglophone" and "Francophone" worlds and a wider regional contrast between these and what is generally known as the "Lusophone," or Portuguese-speaking, African landscape. The purpose is not to serve as a definitive, comprehensive study of poetics in the African continent; rather, it means to set the context for Angolan poetics in terms of artistic expression with regard, either explicitly or implicitly, to language use and its effects on the concept of the nation as conceived by the existing regime.

The chapters that follow will then illustrate a general theory that tasks itself in explaining poetry's proper place in reflecting on this linguistic movement in Angola, as both a consequence of modern historical processes and as an essential piece of this relatively new country's unique nation-building processes. Subsequently, an analysis of the poetry of the period will follow, beginning by looking first from the critical lens of the socially compromised verses socially intimate poetics as previously theorized. This approach evidences an explicit and purposeful intent to suggest an alternative to previously presented perspectives, upon having supplemented these with the less-studied yet certain not less important dimension of language as a critical, and potentially criticized, element of reflection on the process of nation building in Angola from the point of view of the poetry written first during the independence period, and then in the post-independence period. Ultimately, this study posits a relatively precise division between two literary periods, based in large part on the political situation of the country but with a core significance held within the anti-colonial discourse of the pre-independence period. This duality, as hinted earlier, will be reflected in two "phases." The reader will see a "first phase" as an expression of the ideal of "unity through diversity" centered always in a single linguistic framework, and then a "second phase," existing as a counterpoint to the first and in subtle defiance of this sociopolitical and epistemological strategy. In contrast to previous critical schema which rely on a simultaneous evolution of thought, usually depending on a theorizing of communication between differing literary trajectories, this alternative structure basis its approach on a diachronic perspective. Within this frame of reference, one understands the literary as an essential trace function and factor of the overall evolution of the Angolan national psyche of the period, at least as far as the readers of Angolan poetry and students of Angola have come to recognize, study, and comprehend its abundant complexities.

As stated above, before continuing on to the specific case of language use in Angola there must be first a general context upon which to ascribe this study. It is in view of this idea that one begins by contextualizing the phenomenon within the framework of language use (within both a Europeanized and non-Europeanized frame) and institutionally-guided nation building in modern and contemporary sub-Saharan Africa.

The African continent, and in particular, sub-Saharan Africa, possesses the most linguistically varied and rich region on the planet. These languages encompass a variety of language groups, reflecting on the complexity of the intercultural relationships which may seem almost alien to the Occidental mind accustomed to conceiving of Africa as a more monolithic and unilateral cultural matrix. Such a fiction could not be further from the truth.

According to various studies and estimates, the number of languages spoken number in the thousands.[7] The dialectal or familial

---

[7] Scholars have divided these languages, for better or for worse, into four major groups: "Niger-Congo," "Afro-Asiatic," "Nilo-Saharan," and "Khoesan," (also more commonly written as "Khoisan") for a total of approximately 2000 languages (4-9). Of course this is an approximation; the true number of languages (as opposed to dialects of a larger language, as-of-yet unrecorded languages, etc.) continues to elude even the most dedicated scholars on the subject. Although there may exist some evident approximations between different languages, a complication exists at the moment of attempting to classify this myriad of tongues. It is, in fact, difficult to group these languages into families, since in

divisions which they reflect seem to stem from linguistic and somewhat geographic, spatial differentiations and reveal movement over time, as the language families tend to spread into and over the desert "border" between North and sub-Saharan Africa (with the exception of the Khoesan, or Khoisan, language family). Thus, the nature of this linguistically complex region is fluid and not subject to the artificial nature of official borders or boundaries.[8] It is possible to posit that without any extra-continental interference this linguistic plurality would have more than likely continued to evolve down some unknown path toward several more "official" languages, or those a government recognizes for purposes of internal communication and education, as well as a naturally expected myriad of unofficial languages which local governments may or may not recognize and for which there may or may not exist any sort of educational or institutional support. Yet the number of official languages on the continent is few. These are in almost all cases the languages of the former European colonizers whose presence, outside of trade routes which have existed for millennia, has been felt for no more than 500 years (as in the case of the Portuguese or Spanish; the British and French had exercised their occupational latency for much less time). These languages are, for the most part, English, French, Italian (in Ethiopia, which for the most part is in total disuse among all sectors of the population), Portuguese, and (in the case of Equatorial Guinea) Spanish.[9]

---

many cases "the nearest varieties [within dialect clusters] would be mutually intelligible, but not those at a distance from each other. It therefore becomes difficult … to establish a language boundary" (Batibo 2) much less to classify members of a distinct language family.

[8] It is perhaps in part for this reason that the process of appropriation of European languages, and particularly of Portuguese (first as lingua franca, and later on in an attempt to be applied on the population as a more generally spoken language), has occurred.

[9] Arabic and Amharic are official languages of the North and East African countries whose colonial history has been, and will continue to be, the subject of other studies. It should also be noted that Equatorial Guinea has moved toward designating Portuguese another official language of the country, (Embassy, par. 1) further complicating the issue of lingua franca, local languages, and politically-recognized languages (a similar case exists in Mozambique with the incorporation of the country into the British Commonwealth and attempted adoption of English – this will be the focus of a future study).

This movement toward linguistic reduction finds some explanation as part and parcel of an easily evidenced historical process of colonization and hegemonic reaction: in general terms, language use in Sub-Saharan Africa has shifted fundamentally in the past 150 years from an innumerable group of language families divided more or less evenly over the region to continued use of these yet with a preference, a the various institutional levels, given to languages such as English, French, Portuguese, and Spanish. During and after colonial rule there was an explicit attempt to break the diversity of languages spoken through identifiable series of educational and bureaucratic policies installed by the new power brokers in various newly formed countries. Sub-Saharan African governments, since the 1960s, have chosen to present themselves as unified nations. This was done, essentially, as an imitation of the unifying discourse of their former European colonizers whose organizational models these new regimes tended to follow. Policies befitting the discourse then lead to the attempts at eradicating locally and regionally spoken languages not spoken by their former colonizers; it would be upon this population that the new social and ruling elites (many of them being of "creole" origin) had tried to apply the colonizer's language, placing their own identities, in essence, upon those of their respective peoples (Kanana 44-45). The argument that "people's contribution to development can only be realized when the communication barriers are removed ... [a] common language can thus be seen as an integrating force, a means by which participation is facilitated ..." had (and still has) also received acceptance widely, despite the detrimental effects on local languages (46).

The majority of the countries involved in this process had found themselves previously within either the British or French imperial territories; as such, the colonial languages of English and French and their post-colonial treatment would serve as models for providing an initial understanding of earlier and contemporary linguistic policy as well as the attempts at forced linguistic conversion in more recent times.[10] In the case

---

[10] As the reader sees here and throughout the lengthier and more inclusive analysis in this book, the examples given in studies on language politics in the Sub-Saharan African region

of this particular study, the process becomes clear as one delves further into the recent linguistic history of Angola and the more popular and artistic practices of incorporating local language use into the language of the former colonizer continues.[11]

Many educational difficulties have appeared by way of studies of pedagogical practices in Anglophone and Francophone Africa. Policies have tended to center around the use of the official language in schools as the exclusive means of instruction. This has led to some curious results. The most blatant has been that education in languages other than the person's "mother tongue" leads to misperception of high illiteracy rates since the only language measured in national studies of literacy is, of course, the official one (Brock-Utne 485-86). Suggestions to return to the teaching of those "mother tongues" either concomitantly to, or before, the European language official in a given country, has been proposed[12] in

---

come generally from Anglophone and Francophone Africa, rather than from Lusophone Africa, much less from Angola in particular.

[11] One rather preoccupying aspect of Kanana's study is the generalization of "African" language use as extended throughout an area encompassing dozens of separate cultures and countries, each with regional and local sociopolitical strata developing at differing paces in various directions. The article in question, for example, does mention Portuguese; nonetheless, it does so with no citation or other provable information beside very general phrasing such as "the statistics on the success of such an approach are not encouraging" (50) and then including no such statistics in relation to the Portuguese-speaking countries of African (only those within the English or French language spheres). This phenomenon, as such, becomes a rather important point of discussion within this critical context.

[12] Brock-Utne's essay concludes with such a proposal. Harries's article on the use of English and other languages in religious missions in Anglophone Africa also makes such a statement against viewing English as the only measure for literacy and as the only true language of education in the region. "Research has shown that students who engage in their early primary education using mother-tongue end up with a better knowledge of English than do those who are from the beginning taught using English. As in many countries around the world — such as Germany, Holland, etc., English being extremely widely known and used does not mean that it has displaced mother tongue" (281). Kamwangamalu also makes this case, again, in the Anglophone sphere (327). One should pay particular attention to the absence of studies on Lusophone African case studies (with the exception of Severo's study which focuses entirely on policy and linguistic combinations between Portuguese and Kimbundu) in the light of the peripheral placement of the Lusophone in Sub-Saharan Africa.

the past several years. There has also been the tendency to generalize the Anglophone policies as those which may serve as a model for viewing the whole of Sub-Saharan Africa in this area, such as in the case presented by Bamgbose's critical work.[13] One indeed sees that the evidence against such a model exists not only as a facet of the criticism to its fundamental philosophical basis (that of a single, unified theory of language use within a Pan-African socio-historical and synchronic framework), but to the nature of language use as an element of the power structure outside of the Anglophone African context. More specifically, and due to which this study and others akin to it exist, the Lusophone and, of very particular interest, the Angolan situation forces the informed reader and / or critic to face a more nuanced and less clearly defined social and linguistic context.

Alongside education comes the area of artistic (mainly literary) writing which, as I have mentioned, can either support or counter the official push toward linguistic, cultural, or political unity (again, whether or not that unity actually exists, or whether it is appropriate for a particular country-wide situation, I will not explicitly argue here). The field of literary criticism in reference to African artistic production has noted that creative writing in English has burgeoned since decolonization. Despite the already mentioned dialog between languages such as English and French and local languages such as Ibo and Yoruba, "[b]y the end of the 1980s, an African canon of literature in English had emerged and become institutionalized" (Gikandi 9).[14] It may suffice to say that this distinction between the thriving spoken languages in many Sub-Saharan Anglophone and Francophone countries and their literary counterparts,

---

[13] Bamgbose's study, for example, utilizes almost exclusively sample cases from Anglophone countries, then mentions "French, Portuguese, and Spanish" on various occasions without delving further into the matter. This corroborates the previous observation which, when taken alongside this one, reveals a hegemony of the Anglophone and Francophone over the Lusophone. I study this phenomenon in some detail in the next chapter.

[14] It is of paramount importance that the reader note the emphasis on English and French as the principle languages of focus and of inter-canon dialog, with Portuguese-language work marginalized if not utterly ignored.

also apparently thriving, leads not only to a linguistic but also a cultural divide among the social classes which only highlights the existence of literature as an aspect of the more powerful elite. As is evident, in the case of Lusophone Africa, and specifically in that of Angola, that this divide runs both ways; the literary and politically entrenched social elite of the latter, mostly borne from the pre-independence social and bureaucratic classist colonial state, have combined with non-elite linguistic and social elements (many of whom have lost their previously stronger contact with the Kimbundu, Umbundu, and other non-Portuguese speaking communities from outside of the larger, Portuguese-speaking zones, and whose linguistic matrix tends toward *recombination* and outright language adoption rather than a imposed singular, unilateral, and ultimately unacceptable language choice) to form a unique, if not contrived in its earlier stages, Angolan Portuguese dialect group and recent literary tradition based in that rapid linguistic evolution.[15]

In returning to the general overview of Sub-Saharan Africa and the issues surrounding language use, other more subtle clashes have appeared which would also challenge these new states. The independence movements against European colonial powers and, in a general sense, the

---

[15] In the push to transform communication modes of the elite into those of the masses, a question remains which continues to contradict these efforts. Readers of African literatures and students of African cultures are perpetually aware of their existence in the periphery. This bewildering fact becomes a defining force in linguistic politics within the region. "Une-as, a essas fonias todas literárias africanas, os vários tipos de perifericidade. E a língua em que constroem um espaço de identidade é sobretudo uma linguagem cultural, mais do que verbal" (Matta, *Literatura*, 33). (Eng., "All of these African literary "-phones" unite them, these various types of peripheralities. And the language in which they construct a space for identity is above all a cultural language, more than a verbal one.") With the imposition of the European languages as national means of communication (yet counting on very few, if any, actual native speakers of the language also being of recent African ancestry, with the exception of countries like Angola) the greatest identifier of the Sub-Saharan African peoples seems that they ought better to stem from their "national" identities' non-centrality. Another potential area of further study, then, could be to analyze how a particularly exceptional case can begin within the auspices of similar linguistic and cultural formation between countries, and then that formation's sudden turn toward a unique process of linguistic appropriation; insofar as this process may be concerned, it will be the bilateral nature of this nationalizing dynamic which the poetry and / other literary arts of the period will aid in categorizing and explaining.

subsequent push toward political unity within each new country, has had to deal with the implicit struggle of a cultural and political, not only linguistic, legacy which the aforementioned colonial power had left implanted there.[16] With respect to this notion one may return to the aforementioned statements (as summarized by Kanana) that linguistic and other policies (mentioned previously) meant to bring the colonies into a culture more akin to that of the assumed European "motherland" would

---

[16] In the case of the French colonies / new Francophone countries for example, the colonial rulers placed a particular emphasis on bringing "civilization" to the African "barbarian:"

> The various personalities and characters ... are identified by the reports' author in relation to a sliding scale of 'civilization' that positioned European culture at one end of the scale and the non-évolués, Africans who as yet had had little or no exposure to French education and society, at the other end, with particular emphasis and interest being paid to those who are seen as being the most 'successful' in moving themselves towards the European end of the scale. (Griffiths 354)

As such, the French colonial governments took great pains to study and "reform" the various non-French-speaking populations. There reforms, at best, took the shape of interference into cultures which the French themselves neither understood nor took the time to understand. At worst, they resulted in a censuring of cultural and linguistic practices which, as I have noted above, continues in some form to this day.

Among other overarching areas, these included the attempts at stopping the supposedly uncivilized marriage practices of Senegalese men as detrimental to the rights of (certain) women: "Concluding her observations on conjugal relations in the final overview report that she compiled from the seventeen field reports following her return to Dakar in late May 1938, Savineau assessed the position of women as under assault and in urgent need of French intervention. She proposed a "conjugal policy" that would reduce the workload of women and promote their social position. Distinguishing between the modern African woman as wife and the African woman as servant, she characterized the former as the woman who is allowed to greet guests to the home in the "*salon*" alongside her husband. The female servant, meanwhile, has been brought in to substitute the domestic service role of the Westernized woman, and Savineau seems to give no consideration in her evaluation of female 'progress,' to the rights of the latter." (368)

Whether or not the reader of this study agrees with the original practices of these peoples or not is not in question; rather, one may observe the lack of an open dialog toward the colonized and their practices as the principle focus of the scene described here. This invasiveness was not necessarily unique to the French case, although according to these accounts such extremes would have been more prevalent in colonial Francophone Africa.

later on be appropriated by the new Sub-Saharan African governments for their use as a tool for the creation of a political and social hegemony on behalf of the new ruling classes. This would function to create a philosophy of a unified nation while simultaneously excluding a vast majority of the population from any form or social mobility.

It is also more than appropriate to discuss briefly the hints of a Postmodern voice in the literary deconstructions of this implied, linguistically-reduced discourse in Anglophone and Francophone Africa as a point of comparison for what the reader will observe shortly in Lusophone Africa, and in particular, in the case of Angola. In the overall African literary context of the late 20th and early 21st Centuries a major change has occurred thanks to dissolving utopian ideals, the periodic destabilization of local governments, the subsequent questioning of notions of unity and the individual's place within it (based in large part on the phenomena described here), and the presence of relatively inexpensive smartphone technology. The internationalization of African literature, and particularly the novel, has opened the world to happenings on the (Anglophone and Francophone regions of the) continent in a way similar to the arrival of "Magical Realism" from Latin American in the late 1950s and early 1960s. Writers such as Aminatta Forna, from Sierra Leone, and Alain Mabanckou, from Congo, have opened up the gritty and violent realities of a war-torn African landscape to Western readers. The discourse in novels such as *The Memory of Love* or *Broken Glass* (Fr: *Verre Cassé*) (respectively) may be described in multivariate terms, building on an intimate discourse to open up a conversation with works such as the first mentioned here. The speaking more specifically of each work, it has been said of the former that it has tended to:

> [f]ocus on the individual, the civilian, and the ways in which the long-term threat of violence, alongside physical and emotional wounding, reconfigures the daily lives of [its] characters. Such lives, like any others, are necessarily built around deep emotional attachments to companions, many of them sexual in nature. (Norridge 19)

In the case of the latter, a literary work from this period may also forgo the discourse of sexual intimacy, looking more closely at the postcolonial condition as a discourse, concomitant to that of the former novel, of both contradiction and a troubled self-awareness (Cissé 238). It is due to this that *Broken Glass*, in particular, passes further toward the criticism of the literary personage in the context of globalization and the social constructions which continuously attempt to define it:

> Le narrateur distingue, en effet, le voyage comme élément stratégique qui énonce la vision globalisante de l'oeuvre, dessine le statut de l'écrivain-monde. C'est à travers le voyage que la littérature-monde apparaît selon des constructions architecturales : espaces du monde, oeuvres du monde, êtres du monde sont représentés grâce a la traversée imaginaire (247).
>
> (Eng: "The narrator distinguishes, in effect, the voyage as a strategic element which foreshadows the work's globalizing vision, that which designs the world-writer's status. It is by way of the voyage that World Literature appears according to architectural construction: spaces of the world, works of the world, beings of the world are represented thanks to this imaginary traversing.")

Placing the African protagonist into a wider literary context looks to obviate the need for a rewriting not only of the global, but of local cultural development. Concomitantly, the act of deconstructing the nation and the postcolonial globalized self for the sake of fully understanding the complex behavior and contradictory nature of each has become an expected result of these works.[17]

---

[17] Within the realm of technologically based literary work (disseminated via smartphone or other digital devices due to the relatively low cost of these), many writers have turned to the internet both for publicity of their existing works. As an example, in the case of Teju Cole ("https://twitter.com/tejucole") this has become the sole artistic medium utilized. Cole's work manages to create a poetic through the limited medium of a set maximum

The case of Lusophone Africa will share some of the same aspects of this process, at least superficially.[18] In countries such as Angolan and Mozambique, as studied in the following chapter, the initial dissemination of the European language happened through a combination of a bureaucracy installed in the country by the colonial power and the rudimentary education system brought there through public and ecclesiastical means. One may even conclude that, during the first three centuries of Portuguese colonization in sub-Saharan Africa, the linguistic situation went relatively undisturbed. The differences begin to show quickly nonetheless, due on the one hand to the peripheral nature of Portuguese colonization relative to that of other European colonizers and, on the other, to a process of both forced and self-selected linguistic appropriation during the independence and post-independence periods.

Ultimately, it is the language's wider spread throughout all social classes in the late 19th and early 20th Centuries, particularly in Angola, and the contradiction of unity concomitant to diversity that it represents, on which the primary focus of this study will reside. The function of Portuguese became one of sociopolitical importance, as an element which speaks to the issues of an ideal of national unity, and its counterargument, the reality of cultural and linguistic plurality and potential disunity. In subsequent chapters, I highlight the poetic expression / reflection on language's place within the wider literary discourse. This multidisciplinary and broader basis has revealed, with the aid of a detailed analysis of key poetic figures and their work, a deeper (and in many cases troubling) relationship between language and people that defines the Angolan a

---

number of keyed letters, spaces, and number in the Twitter system. His work, nonetheless, has become very widely disseminated in Anglophone Africa and has a strong following (DiGiacomo, 2014).

[18] A note on technology: although I will not delve into the use of Twitter and Facebook by writers such as Ondjaki to disseminate their work, on a less invasive level the technological facets of the literary world, such as on-line publishing and the use of social media in maintaining a readership, have gained evermore prominence in the overall literary atmosphere of Lusophone Africa. I discuss this aspect of contemporary literature in Angola and in Luso-Africa in the conclusions to this study.

national concept and epistemology of self-identification in the contemporary period.

Chapter I: *A Sociopolitical Background for Angola and Lusophone Africa*

No one can deny the growing importance of Angola in the Southern African Sphere. In the past decade the country has moved from a post-civil-war situation to one of providing a measure of regional stability and of an imposition authority locally. In purely economic terms, for example, according to data taken from the World Bank, while Portugal (the former colonial "motherland") is moving slowly out of recession, "[Angola] now enjoys growth rates of between 5% and 15%" (Gatinois, par 3). Although the country has taken great strides in gaining recognition within its regional context, as well as becoming a focal point for world attention, the complexities of varied and contradictory notions of "Angolan-ness" have continued to pervade the national consciousness. These are borne from above and below, from the voice of the relatively very oppressive political regime and from the voice of the people, usually with each heard in evident dissonance with the other. The universality of the country's image as extended to the outside and expressed top-down internally has not matched with the happenings within the country itself over the past several decades since independence.

As such, one enters into a sort of debate around issues of Angolan identity in either a "Pan-African," a "Luso-African," or a "Luso-Angolan" context, with elements of each in common or in conflict. The spread of the Portuguese language has complicated matters further, particularly as one delves into the implied arguments which feed off of historical and literary processes. Poetic voices within Angola, when standing together as well as vis-à-vis other similar voices rooted in other Luso-African and non-Luso-African countries, take on the tone of a discussion on the evolution of language use in establishing an Angolan nationality in a post-Colonial and hybridized culture, rather than a more simplified study on intranational political priorities or that of the individual in isolation from his/her sociopolitical context (such as has been the case according to one previously mentioned critical voice). Given the phenomenon outlined previously concerning the attempts at spreading the English and French languages in the Anglophone and Francophone African spheres (respectively), the move beyond superficial appearances which defines the dissemination of Portuguese in Angola will serve as evidence of its historical and sociopolitical uniqueness which has gone mostly unrecognized both within the Luso-African and Lusophone contexts, and particularly outside of this sociocultural and literary matrix. The process of building a unified, national symbolism (from the point of view of those colonized by, as well as the new colonizer of, the Portuguese language) within the relatively new national framework, as both consequence and stimulus to the changes seen in the country since before independence to today, also becomes palpable. This is the message which this chapter discusses as part and parcel of a now re-visited official discourse which both promises a national identity and attempts to silence (or to a degree marginalize) those identities not approved under the scheme.[19] As such, and as the reader observes in the course of this study, the writings of Agostinho Neto, António Jacinto, Ana Paula Tavares, and Luís Kandjimbo will play an essential role in determining the artistic expression of this discourse's parameters. In the work of the latter, within the poem's semiotic the use of mimetic deconstruction may either brashly or diplomatically undermine the official discourse's authority; the works of all four poets, when taken as evidence of a rapid transformation from one artistic viewpoint to another, will also reveal themselves, individually and in conjunction, as an essential moment of reflection on the social and literary construct engendered from the of the overall process of nation building in contemporary Angola. These authors in particular, more so that many others whose work would be available for a study such as this one, embody the use of language, and in particular, of the Portuguese language (whether in combination with other languages, as part of a larger

---

[19] As Basto states, there has been in post-independence Angola the tension between official, institutional discourse and the perspective of the literary elite. "Notons, cependant, dans le paysage culturel angolais ... une contradiction entre une faible affirmation institutionnelle ... et, d'autre part, una maturité evidente de ces écritures littéraires nationales ... " (455). Although her study focuses on prose rather than poetry, and in particular, on notions of narrative multiplicity in Angolan and Mozambican novel, the excision between writer and state, within a context of language use as either an explicit or an implicit institutional marker of citizenship, serves to support the study of particular poetic works here.

dialectal distinction, or in no codified combination with other Angolan languages) as a fundamental aspect of Angolan national identity, insofar as their discussion is based explicitly or implicitly on the language of the former colonizer and current urban, suburban, or semi-rural populations.

The importance of the Portuguese Language as an identity marker outside of the Lusophone World has become more palpable in the past few decades with increasing links identified between Luso-African poets from the late colonial and post-colonial periods and non-Luso-African poets. As an example, Memory Chirere, in her well-known column on Zimbabwean poets from the 1980s, found the assertion that "through [Bvuma's "Real Poetry" from *And NOW the Poets speak* (1981)], one recalls the more prominent Angolan war poet, Agostinho Neto" (par. 5) to be a truism in contemporary African cultural self-reflection. In the same journalistic piece the following verses from the poem "The Real Poetry" appear, revealing to what extent elements from Lusophone African history have become part of the greater discourse of independence and hope:

> It was engraved in killings in Kitanga,
>
> In the betrayals of Mau-Mau,
>
> In the countless anti-people coups.
>
> Its beat was the bones in Bissau
>
> Its metaphors massacres in Mozambique
>
> Its alliterations agony in Angola
>
> Its form and zenith
>
> Fighting in Zimbabwe.
>
> (v. 5-12)

...

Not a private paradise

Nor an individual inferno

But the pain and pleasure

Of People in Struggle.

Viva o Povo!

(v. 21-5)

Bvuma's Pan-African view seems to move its focus toward what may best be codified as a Lusophone identity while also speaking of both historical periods (colonial and Post-colonial) mentioned above. The verse in Portuguese in which the poem reaches culmination has an interesting connotation. Although Bvuma wrote in English in order to facilitate dissemination of his work, the use of Portuguese as a marker of national / extra-national identification of Guinea-Bissau, Mozambique, and Angola calls the reader's attention to a linguistic peculiarity of these countries. That is, the immediate identification of these African spaces with the Portuguese language (as opposed to one of counter-position to the English, French, or in direct affirmation of and reference to a language such as Kimbundu, etc.) does not preclude their inclusion in an essentially non-European discourse. The reader may find the assumed association of Agostinho Neto with both the Portuguese language and anti-colonial revolutions in Africa rather ubiquitous; yet, this separate Luso-African identity based in many ways on the use of the former colonizer's language which was established as a national one in 1960s and 70s through Neto's poems, also being Neto's primary language. (As is evidenced in this study, one of the most notable identifiers of his poetic voice is the incorporation of the most widely-spoken local language from which his party, thee MPLA, was borne. In his work, words and phrases from Kimbundu have found themselves combined with Portuguese, although not necessarily in an act of code-switching.[20]) This perhaps unexpected appearance of Portuguese as a language associated with other African (in this case, specifically Angolan) cultural and linguistic practices points toward a general linguistic phenomenon in the former Portuguese colonies in contemporary Africa. While the so-called Anglophone and Francophone countries use English and French, respectively, as a sort of lingua-franca, the Lusophone countries seem to possess a higher percentage of both second language and actual *native speakers* of Portuguese not of European descent. As Helena Dali explains when referencing the African colonial use of other Western European languages in comparison to Portuguese:

> Por el contrario, en el portugués de las colonias africanas se evidencia una fuerte tendencia al mono- o polilingüismo vernacular, cuyo resultado es la criollización manifiesta en todos los niveles sociales (en mayor o menor grado …) y a través de todas las vías de comunicación, tanto en la tradición oral como en la expresión escrita. Desde muy temprano se vislumbra el cuño africano en la lengua y la cultura lusas … A nivel del léxico, la lengua portuguesa se ve enriquecida por un gran número de vocablos de origen africano, en su mayoría provenientes del 'quimbundu', lengua bantú de la región del Congo, y de uso bastante común.(287-88)

("On the contrary, in the Portuguese of the African colonies a strong tendency toward monolingualism and vernacular polyglotism is evidenced, the result of which is the creolization manifest at all social levels (in greater or lesser gradations …) and by way of all means of communication, as much in oral tradition as in written expression. Since early on the African crib was surmised within the Luso language and culture … On the lexical level, the Portuguese language was seen as enriched by a great number of words of African origin, a majority stemming from

---

[20] This trend continues in Tavares' poetry, not at all in Jacinto's, and then present in that of Kandjimbo in a few limited but for a few very notable occurrences.

"Kimbundu," a Bantu language from the Congo region, and in common use.")

Such "vernacular polyglotism" and "criolization" have happened as a general rule of the monolingual development of the Lusophone countries to a greater or lesser degree. As shown above, Angola's process of linguistic evolution has centered on lexical incorporation as opposed to a true creolizing process (such as is the case of Cape Verde or Guinea-Bissau). This simply has not happened in Anglophone or Francophone Africa.[21]

Although Dali retains a notably Eurocentric perspective, those being summarized under the colonizer's voice as it were, the issue of the language's widely recognized use as the principle language of the population of Lusophone Africa (whether as secondary to a creole based on Portuguese or as a native language of large numbers of the population) is not a dubious one. It is, nonetheless, a statement problematized by certain implications based on the assumed superiority of the "Luso," or Portuguese language based, linguistic and cultural elements, as opposed to the "local." Put another way, one may see a tension between an imagined cultural centrality in opposition to the cultural diversity which more evidently defines the region (Matta 31-32).[22]

In this, yet more aspects of the discussion of language recognition as an integral part of national identity in Lusophone Africa begin to

---

[21] As mentioned previously in this study, educational preferences have focused attention on the "purer" forms of each language and have largely ignored local languages or vernaculars.

[22] Madureira's study on the applicability of Santos' theories of Lusophone identities, or the "Calibanized Prospero," is also a point at which both the similarities in individual behavior of colonial masters and the differences in overall relationships between those "masters" and their contracted subjects become clear (204-07). The complexities of the case of colonization, decolonization, and post-colonial state building in countries such as Angola and Mozambique, although similar on the surface to those of Anglophone and Francophone Africa, possess marked differences in realization as Madureira discusses in his study.

appear. Alongside the sociopolitical argument, it is preferable to note also that in even the most contemporary of critical works on African literatures and poetics, one may find the mention of the Portuguese and the use of their language, along with the English, French, Dutch, etc., on the part of non-European descendant Africans as what Diop calls and "undisturbed denial of self" (23).[23] In fact, when referring to the "European" colonizers, in many cases critics will indicate a specific period, "late nineteenth and early twentieth century" (Kasfir 59), or a specific language, as is the case with Owomoyela's focus on African identity as expressed through "a deep immersion in European languages" (10) with a continuous relation of "European" meaning "English" (45-6). These and many other critics, including but not limited to the aforementioned and very recent article by Mirabeau, work by Tala,[24] and a short chapter on "Pan-African Agenda in Languages" by Omotoso and Dennis which discusses Yoruba in the community of African descendants of London (46), while valid in their discussions of particular phenomena related to their respective areas of expertise, seem to ignore the longevity (as historical possibility and / or as having ever happened at all) of Portuguese colonial presence in Africa. This, of course, lends itself as one of many factors (as mentioned above) which lead to the high number of native speakers of Portuguese in the former Portuguese colonies in Africa, and their peoples' eventual self-inclusion (whether by choice or by necessity) within what many refer to as the Lusophone World (*A Lusofonia*).[25] [Even more objective sources such as those providing

---

[23] Curiously, Diop's very powerful examples come entirely from former English or French colonial contexts (25-7) (and as such, ironically negate the presence of those of the Portuguese-speaking countries within what he and others have considered the African post-colonial context).

[24] This is a reference to Kashim Tala's 1999 book *Orature in Africa* which Mirabeau also aptly cites.

[25] Batibo has even stated that the privileging of English over local languages has happened in "Cameroon, Mozambique, ..." (19). Although correct in the sense that Mozambique has joined the British Commonwealth (and thus remains the only known non-English speaking country to have done so), such an error of over-generalization serves to highlight the liminal place of Portuguese in the contemporary Africanist critical mindset.

information for the internationally recognized *Background Notes* series state that, despite the existence of various other languages in Angola, "Portuguese is both the official and predominant language" (2).[26] This comes in contrast to the use of another European language in a country known as part of the larger, "Francophone" World, Senegal, where the same source cites that: "French is the official language but is used regularly only by the literate minority" (*Background Notes ... Senegal*, 3).[27]]

Arenas has pointed out this unintended marginalization on the part of the Anglophone and Francophone African states in his study on contemporary Angolan literature, within his discussion on the place of Luso-African letters in the world socio-literary hegemony:

> [T]he chronic peripheral condition of most sub-Saharan Africa in economic and political terms has contributed significantly to the marginalization of its cultural production as a whole on the world scene. This dynamic is quite palpable in the case of Lusophone African literatures, which have remained obscured by virtue of being both African and written in Portuguese. (*Lusophone*, 160-1)

Even in the culture of literary criticism outside of Africa this obscurity remains. The best-known organization representing literatures in all major and minor languages, the Modern Language Association, does not necessarily find itself immune to the effects of the unseen Luso-African self:

> Francophone and anglophone [sic] African literatures have been represented in MLA divisions and on panels for some decades now, and they constitute a 'canonical' corpus of African texts in a

---

[26] Again, a very general source of information, based on the data shown previously in this study, reveals an understanding of the difference in linguistic terms between the majority of Sub-Saharan African countries and the Lusophone African group of countries.

[27] It is also of note that studies such as that conducted by Clegg and Afitska on the use of European languages in «African Classrooms» focuses solely on examples from so-called «Anglophone» countries.

colonial language; but lusophone [sic] and hispanophone [sic] African literatures are practically invisible, although writers such as Paula Tavares, Mia Couto, and Juan Tomás Ávila Laurel deserve to be better known. (Lionnet 219)

Sousa Santos has also commented on this phenomenon as part of a wider peripheral place of the Lusophone World, for reasons of economic imposition (or lack thereof) over the Portuguese colonies, the status of Portugal as a neo-colonial possession of British economic power, as well as for linguistic ones:

> while the British Empire was based on a dynamic balance between colonialism and capitalism, the Portuguese Empire was based on an equally dynamic imbalance between and excess and a deficit of colonialism.
>
> As regards colonial discourses, the subalternity of Portuguese colonialism resides in the fact that, since the seventeenth century, the history of colonialism has been written in English, not Portuguese. ("Between Prospero and Caliban," 11)

The perspective expressed above is concerned less with the status of the peoples living in the colonies and Portuguese colonial behavior in Africa, and much more on the status of the colonial center, Portugal, relative to other European powers in Africa.[28] Yet the overall perspective on the hegemony between these colonial powers, one in which the British had utilized Portugal and, as such, viewed the latter's empire also as inferior, has evidently lent itself to a similar structure of authority within postcolonial Africa. In other words, Santos' seemingly Eurocentric focus does not in any way weaken the argument, as such, when facing the

---

[28] Liebig traces this notion when speaking of the constructs of "Knowledge and Power," in the sense which Foucault gives them, in the way through which Afro-Brazilian writers do not seem to appear with any sort of prominence in the American / African-American critical eye, outside of the linguistic limitations of the latter (23-24).

marginal status of the Lusophone relative to the other major literary and sociopolitical communities on the African continent.[29]

While these somewhat more universally accepted voices have described and, as could be argued, may have actually created and maintained a sort of liminal existence for the Portuguese-speaking nations within the contemporary African context (Burness, *Fire*, xi), the presence of the Portuguese language and Luso-African peoples' unique links to the rest of the Lusophone world (Brazil, Portugal, etc.) allow both inclusion in the greater post-colonial Africa as well as the distinguishing of their hybrid and complex national and regional identities. The language has, essentially and despite the detrimental effects it has had on other languages (particularly in the case of Angola), allowed access to the modern world through its imposition on its unwitting colonial subjects. "A imposição da língua portuguesa à amálgama étnico-cultural ... cria ao mesmo tempo condições para a inexistência da glotofagia e dramas linguísticos, transformando a língua de dominação exógena em língua de libertação e de acesso à modernidade ... " (Abreu 99). (Eng "The Portuguese language's imposition onto the ethic-cultural matrix ... creates at the same time conditions for the inexistence of glotophagy and linguistic drama, transforming the language of exogenous domination into the language of freedom and one of access to modernity ..."). In such a context of bilateral interaction, the oppressor can easily find itself appropriated; the Portuguese language, as a symbol and tool of the oppressor, can thus become the root of a new freedom. In short, and in terms of language use in the Luso-African sphere, one principle figure in Contemporary Angola has stated that "todos os povos ... apropriaram-se do Português" (Kandjimbo, *Entrevista*, min. 1) (Eng., "all of our peoples ... have appropriated Portuguese"), and that along with this assertion comes the knowledge that these among these same peoples "existem outras línguas" (min. 2) (Eng., "other languages exist").

---

[29] The situation becomes even more complex when looking at the reciprocal neo-colonization of Lusophone countries between each other. Angola's notable heavy investment in various areas of Portugal's economy has come as a reminder of the latter's precarious place within the concrete, hegemonic structures of the Portuguese-speaking world's sociopolitical matrix (Gatinois, par 1-10).

Yet one cannot simply or innocently accept the notion of a "Lusofonia literária" (Matta, *Literatura*, 30) without realizing the simplification this notion implies.[30] By removing the non-Lusophone / non-Portuguese cultural basis for the literatures involved, the reader clearly runs the risk of reducing to nothing that which makes the texts readable to both African and extra-African audiences. One may also find that the African otherness actually becomes more acute when written in Portuguese by the simple fact, as noted elsewhere in this study, that the Portuguese language itself is peripheral in the world language system (30), as previously commented. It is at this point one may again emphasize that, even in post-colonial Africa, the language becomes a third wheel of the Anglo-Franco literary and sociocultural bicycle; it exists, yet its nature looks so unlike what the others have experienced that it either becomes subsumed into an inappropriate Pan-Africanist matrix (which itself stands as yet another simplification, as shown earlier in this study) or entirely ignored. The former possibility relates to the poetic citation at the beginning of this chapter – Neto's words ring acutely in the postcolonial, Sub-Saharan African ear, yet the deeper meaning behind it becomes lost from the desire to make all voices in the region seem less diverse and, as such, more alike. As I have also clarified, the latter happens more on a daily basis in popular and academic media, whether through simple ignorance of the Lusophone's implicit marginalization within such circles or by choice, with the evident focus on English and French (simultaneously with an emphasis on the cultures which utilize these languages) and their richly networked process of dissemination.

Ultimately the linguistic and cultural identities of the Portuguese-speaking world are as complex and misunderstood as they are controversial. Here I have spoken both generally on language in Lusophone Africa as compared with other "Africas," and have placed

---

[30] It should also be observed that, in the introduction to Afolabi and Burness' 2003 edited collection of essays by several scholars in the field of Lusophone African literatures, these two authors have made a case for the sort of separation of the post-colonial literary Lusophone identity which the present study describes, particularly in the areas of blending local languages and cultures with those of the former colonizer (3-4).

some, very appropriate focus on the country of study here, namely, Angola. The study may now delve further into this web of language, nationality, and poetry in this very specific and dynamic case.[31]

Conversely it is evident that the process exists in a bilateral matrix (an aspect which very much differentiates the Luso-African experience from the Anglophone or Francophone ones). A similar confluence of the European becoming African, or the africanization of a European self, in other Luso-African nations besides Angola, both from poets whose ancestry one may classify as "African" (whose parentage does not stem from Europe) and poets whose parentage does stem from Europe, becomes visible.[32] As an example, Rui Knopfli, the child of Portuguese immigrants in Mozambique (whose genetic heritage may be found in his Swiss roots), composed the following verses in his poem "Naturalidade" (Eng., "Naturalness"):

Europeu, me dizem.

---

[31] The general outlook for languages in Africa, whether historically established or more recent arrivals, seems relatively complex. In some exemplary situations various languages can cohabitate in a geographic space to some degree. In others, one language or a handful of languages will dominate the linguistic landscape. Of course this does not happen in isolation of other processes; as I have shown thus far, languages spread with peoples, ideologies, and historical influences and confluences. In Angola in particular, these have related directly to: the spread and establishment of the colonizer's peoples as traders or clergy into multiple geographic regions corresponding to variety of already stabilized cultures in the country; the constructed political structures surrounding a somewhat racially integrated (although very elitist) bureaucracy; the creation of a society encompassing various levels of social class and stratification consistent with such a bureaucracy; and a literary production based on the colonizer's language (one which has shown an admirable flexibility and capacity for adaptation in incorporating a plethora of vocabulary and structures from the previously spoken languages of its newest speakers). I have analyzed these elements from within a diachronic critical orientation. The "African" person, in many ways, becomes in part "European;" this person then goes on to help rule a new country, taking advantage of historical processes to enhance this hybrid identity and foment its dissemination across vast areas.

[32] Inocência Matta discusses the notion of a Pan-Lusophone linguistic and cultural construct as both destructive to independent nations in Africa and as necessary for the kind of cross-cultural discourse on which such cultures depend (*Literatura*, 29-32).

Eivam-me de literatura e doutrina

europeias

e europeu me chamam.

Não sei se o que escrevo tem a raiz de algum

pensamento europeu.

É provável ... Não, é certo,

mas africano sou.

Pulsa-me o coração ao ritmo dolente

desta luz e deste quebranto.

Trago no sangue uma amplidão

de coordenadas geográficas e mar Índico.

Rosas não me dizem nada,

caso-me mais à agrura das micaias

e ao silêncio longo e roxo das tardes

com gritos de aves estranhas.

Chamais-me europeu? Pronto, calo-me.

Mas dentro de mim há savannas de aridez

e planuras sem fim

com longos rios langues e sinuosos,

uma fita de fumo vertical,

um negro e uma viola estalando.

    (*Antologia*, 210)

(Eng:

European, they tell me.

They infect me with European

literature and doctrines

and they call me European.

I don't know if what I am writing is rooted in some

European thought.

It's probable … no, it's certain,

yet I am African.

The heart in me pulses to the pained rhythm

of this light and this weakness.

I carry in my blood the ampleness

of geographic coordinates and the Indian Ocean.

Roses tell me nothing,

I'm linked to the Sickle bush's[33] bitterness

and to the prolonged and violet silence of afternoons

with the cries of strange birds.

You call me European? Fine, I'll be quiet.

Yet within me there are arid savannahs

and endless plains

with long, languid, sinuous rivers,

a vertical, smoky ribbon,

a black man and a crackling viola.)[34]

Although accused of Euro-Centrism later in life (Nielson 96), the type of self-incorporation into the poeticized body into the greater body of the African landscape, coupled with the bi-continental identity of "European" and "African" as a synchronous (although not necessarily harmonious[35]) union as seen here represents part of the unique Luso-

---

[33] The «micaia», or «sickle bush», is a plant found specifically in the South Eastern region of Africa.

[34] All translations are by the author of this study, unless otherwise noted.

African discourse. This unexpected, dual self-identification nascent in the poetry of António Jacinto and more prevalent in that of Luís Kandjimbo, the latter having come from a socio-historical framework converse to that of the former, will become evident.[36] The reader will also see the poetic expression of the contradictions in its engendering, a product of an oppressive political regime and the utopian philosophy upon which it had built its power base.

---

[35] Hamilton speaks of the way in which Knopfli shows "sensitivity to the tensions inherent to the situation in Mozambique" as well as the way "the social condition in Mozambique is multifaceted" (*Voices*, 194). It is this lack of simplification which makes his work, and this poem, an appropriate introduction and moment of transition to themes of race, class, and language found not only in his home country but also in Angola.

[36] It is also important to note the physical manifestations of this very unusual union in literature. António Jacinto's *Fábulas de Sanji* (Eng.: *Fables of Sanji*) includes a short section of «Explicações» (Eng. «Explanations») which identifies the particularly Angolan terms and linguistic structures found in various fables from the second part of the work (24). This converts the text from a «pure» work of literature into a didactic book, teaching Angolan national heritage through (supposedly) popular stories as well as the peculiarities of the Angolan-Portuguese language in which those stories are now expressed.

Chapter II: *History and Poetry in Contemporary Angola*

The sociopolitical sphere has shaped Angolan literature since the beginnings of the ideology of Angolan independence in the end of the 19th Century, during which time only a nascent concept of an Angola not under the Portuguese yoke was emerging. A desire to have Angolan cultural independence recognized, although not having yet consolidated into a true movement at that time, did begin to show itself through literary expression. From this, it is obvious that the ideal of a relatively unified, literary voice which flowed concomitantly alongside social and political change bore the notion that "a literatura, no nosso país, sempre acompanhou o Movimento de Libertação Nacional" (Kandjimbo, "A Dimensão," 69). As Hamilton has suggested, "[t]he revolutionary vanguard's cultural resistance, with its posturing and stylistic aberrations, is in itself and emotional-ideological component of the larger effort to overthrow the existing political order" ("Posturing," 160). This is particularly apparent insofar as the discussion of the time period under consideration here would encompass.

As such, it is possible to see the existing theories of a development of a literature of Angolan expression within a greater anti-colonialist discussion (which a discourse against such a simplistic unifying perspective would later subvert), as well as to expound on their mutual exchange. The first is the historical versus the personal within a parallel spatial framework. There appear to be, according to this approach first conceived from the writings of Inocência Matta, two principle areas of poetic discourse in the poetry of Angola as it has developed over the past century and a half. They seem to run in confluence. One is the socially compromised trajectory, whose intimacy the poetry does not necessarily express; the other, the intimate experience of the social, in which the poetic voice / poetic subject finds encapsulated the ontological within a greater epistemological structure of his or her social context (*Literatura*, 23). Beginning in the late 19th Century and continuing on, "... fez-se, pois, um longo percurso: a retórica do discurso identitário (angolano) polarizará, doravante, uma bissemia: a dimensão épica e a dimensão construtiva" (96). (Eng., "a long course was taken: the rhetoric of the discourse of (Angolan) identity would polarize, from here on, bissemically: the epic dimension and the constructive dimension.") In this sense, the poetic reflecting an ontological framework for social liberation and, later on, the disenchantment engendered from this discourse's failures, finds its equilibrium with the "epic;" the somewhat more individually-oriented poetry of the subject within the social context, in essence, tethers the hybrid state of the single to that the individual and / or communal. The latter, a process of identity building, then allows a "constructive" poetry to occur.

Before continuing an analysis of poetic trajectories, it will be useful to discuss the roots of a language-based analysis of the poetic discourse that follows. That is, it has become considered common knowledge that, at least as of c. 2008, "cerca de 7,5 milhões de habitantes (entre 12,5)" (Clavis, par. 1) (Eng., "almost 7.5 million inhabitants (from among 12.5)") of Angola speak Portuguese.[37] There is even data to support the notion that up to 60% of all Angolans, along with virtually the whole of the urban populations in Luanda, Benguela, and all other cities and large towns in the country, have adopted the Portuguese language as their primary means of communication both at work and at home ("Portuguese", par. 1). This is also reported according to a study of the Ministry of Education's 2003 data collection efforts (Severo 26).[38] Other projections estimate that up to 60% of Angolans speak the language as their primary language outside of the home, while only 40% use the language as their "L1," or mother tongue (Halme 260). Other data sources

---

[37] The use of an internet reference here, although based on data collected from official channels, is meant to illustrate to what extent this number is accepted as "correct." This may or may not be easily refuted, depending on the sources, strength, and relative appeal of the various other data shown here and elsewhere.

[38] Severo's studies on the creation of the Angolan dialects of Portuguese based on a Bakhtian approach to multilingualism and language as part of a power structure outline many of the regime's official discourse. These are useful as studies of the legal aspects of language use and power in contemporary Angola.

may exist both anecdotally and semi-officially in the near or conceivable future which would aid in providing further evidence one way or another.

In any case, and as is perceivable in this brief summary, in the course of realizing the insurmountable task of collecting and processing such large amounts of information various official and academic entities, and other professionals, have come up with results which differ very concretely from one another. There exists yet another study which states that fewer than 60,000 Angolans actually speak Portuguese, the rest speaking exclusively Kimbundu, Umbundu, Kicongo, as well as a myriad of other languages (Inverno 203).[39] As such, although the majority of studies, commentaries, and other sources put the number of native speakers at around 50 to 60 percent, there seems to be no solid and unbiased census or other data (such as that one may expect from countries such as Portugal or the United States) on the actual percentage of the real number of native, second language, or other classifications of speakers of Portuguese in Angola.

There exists, beyond the historical process of urbanization and movements of internal refugees within Angola during the civil wars period (an issue which will be discussed shortly), also a now recognized and much more recent linguistic appropriation process. The parameters of this new phenomenon will reside with historical processes of language adoption in Angola, as the younger generations in and outside of the urban areas have continued to adopt the Portuguese language to the detriment of languages such as Umbundu and Kwanyama (languages which for these speakers would not be of much practical use in the new national context) (Halme 261).[40] All of the languages named here have

---

[39] Inverno's study, beyond the description summarized above, compares plural formation in Angolan and Brazilian Portuguese as a consequence of phonological stratification. One should note that the data on language use dates from the 1980s, a period in which the language was still expanding into what more recent studies and data collection have attempted to indicate as the present-day linguistic and cultural space which the Portuguese language occupies.

[40] In the wider Lusophone Sphere a similar process is happening as well in Mozambique, with evermore members of each generation losing their ties to the older languages in the

been found in a constant state of flux in any case, keeping the notion of a consistent percentage of speakers a theoretical construct only and a real world impossibility. It is logical, in any case, to join this phenomenon with the language's official place as a unifying factor in the creation of a national identity, not only on the part of the Angolan government but also on the part of each Lusophone African country's government within the "postcolonial national project" (Arenas, *Lusophone*, 160).

Returning briefly to poetics, the arts also played a central role in determining the linguistic future of the country. In terms of the literature produced during the period, it is written almost entirely in Portuguese. Although a small group of poems published in other languages exists, even in recent times those poems have been disseminated along with their Portuguese-language translations (Marques 25-60).[41] Essentially this means that, while readers may appreciate and even somewhat understand the other languages, the vast majority will prefer to read the texts in Portuguese. This is a testament to the results and consequences of the re-acculturation process described above: the relative importance of Portuguese has become emphasized to the point at which writers know that their work will not gain a readership, even internally, unless written in this formerly colonial language (Arenas, *Lusophone*, 117).

The combination of all of the factors mentioned has ultimately aided in creating a linguistic environment in which virtually all populations within the country (at least in theory if not in practice, to which the residents of Lusophone African countries, and particularly Angola and Mozambique, may attest) have not only adopted Portuguese, they have

country for various socioeconomic or political reasons. As will become apparent later on in this study, this process has not happened there with the same speed or with the same underlying causes as in Angola.

[41] Marques' newer anthology of Angolan Poetry is, by far, the most complete of its kind. However, insofar as it includes poetry written in Kimbundu, it ensures through translation that these poems are readable, and as such, that the book is appealing, to the majority audience in the country. Due to the lack of an appropriate critical introduction one can assume that the book was written for a readership well-versed in the local genre of the period.

also taken possession of this formerly European language to a measurable extent. Whether on purpose, as the Angolan elite governing class would desire, or as a means of survival and a tool to thrive in the post-independence era, the language serves as a potentially nationally unifying force, much more so that in all other Sub-Saharan African countries with the exception of South Africa.[42] As such, the use of the language as both an internal and external marker of this unique group of post-colonial identities in African would find a logical place within Angola and contemporary Africa.

Before continuing in a discussion on poetry, it is absolutely essential to study also, and in more detail, the historical processes leading up to the current cultural, socio-epistemological, and linguistic discussion. Pires Laranjeira's 1989 work, although pertaining to a somewhat dated perspective, gives some indications of the challenges faced by the Angolan (and other Luso-African) peoples during the formative years of the independence movements during which there was an attempt at the "… redescoberta das raízes civilizacionais africanas e pela descoberta de caminhos universais para a recuperação da dignidade pessoal, da autonomia regional e da independência nacional…" (66) (Eng. "rediscovery of African civilizations' roots and the discovery of universal paths toward the recuperation of personal dignity, regional autonomy, and national independence"). This is visible as a first, necessary step away from the self-identification as a culture suffering under the colonizer's yoke and toward the ideal of a self-incorporation into the new nation-state. Yet, even then the notion of nationhood based on colonial-period border divisions in Southern Africa had begun to surface:

> Desde o início da década de 50, a recepção dessas novas literaturas processou-se de um modo descontínuo e diferido, pelas consabidas razões de ordem política, mas a quantidade e a diversidade, tanto de texto literários como críticos e antologias,

---

[42] As studied in the next chapter and mentioned briefly above, the linguistic recombination of Portuguese with Kimbundu, creating a very specific set of dialects in Angola, reinforces this seemingly sweeping statement.

recitais e traduções, implicam, desde logo, um conceito de *sistematicidade nacional.* (71)

(Eng: "From the beginning of the 1950s, the receiving of these new literatures was processed in a discontinuous and differed way, by way of common knowledge reasoning of a political order, yet the number and variety, as much of literary as of critical texts and anthologies, open air readings and translations, imply, of course, a concept of *national systematization*").

This *systematization* begins at the level of textual groupings, moving then toward a more focused process of nation building through language (as seen in other regions of Sub-Saharan Africa) and through acculturation in the independence and post-independence, civil war periods. Literature begins to makes known its essential role in the first steps toward creating and expressing a national consciousness to replace that of a colonial and / or colonized view of self. Subsequently, one may also see that the basis in a thematic process of self-discovery and in forming a concept of *nation*, at least within the broader social context, even before the chaos of that post-independence era in contemporary Luso-African literatures, had not gone unrecognized.

From a broader Lusophone African view, the national identities of the residents of these countries, insofar as the official discourse of each country wishes to propagate these identities linguistically, find a common bond through their appropriation of the Portuguese language as their own.[43] In the very specific case of Angola, this process of acculturation of the Portuguese language to fit the new Angolan identity has left Angola

---

[43] It is on this note that I (and others) would argue toward Portuguese as not only a European and American (i.e., Brazilian) language, but also, given the evolution of the language in a relatively independent manner in these countries, as an African one. Arenas makes hint to this notion when speaking of the linguistic complexity and "richness" of Ondjaki's prose (*Lusophone,* 180). Given this, and as I will continue to argue here, the ideal of plurality as secondary to a Lusophone identity within the Luso-African countries, and for the present case, in Angola, may come under scrutiny by the same defenders of the discourse whose social and political positions within Angolan society rely almost entirely on such a simplistic notion.

with a very distinct form of Portuguese, one which has been called an "'Angolan' Portuguese language" (Chabal, "Aspects," 27). This dialect of the Portuguese language, according to a recent study, began in the "musseques" ("slums") and became more widely spoken over time throughout the country (27-8). The cultural nuances and consequences of such a process will become clearer through the analysis of writers whose poetry, when viewed from within both a metaphoric and a socio-linguistic framework, serves as vital to this expressive evolution. By way of such a process, then, they themselves become key figures in this new, socio-linguistic understanding of Angolan literary and cultural development.

In historical terms, the language entered what is now Angola along with the first Portuguese explorers in the 16th Century. Both linguistically and geographically, the Portuguese penetrated the interior of the territory for the first several centuries of the colonial period. Expansion did not really occur in fact until the 19th Century, when commercial, military and political pressure on the part of the Portuguese forced the use of the language further into the relatively uncharted (from the perspective of the Portuguese) colonial lands. This extension on the part of the colonial power coincided with the establishment, proliferation, and continued presence of Catholic missions in Lusophone Africa:

> Four-hundred and seventy years of missionary work on African soil — mainly south of the Sahara: from Cape Verde, Sierra Leone, and the ancient kingdom of the *Kongo*, to the lands of the Cape of Good Hope and thence, to the Great Zimbabwe, Mozambique, and the Swahili coast (up to present-day Somalia), Eritrea, and Ethiopia — are thus the result of the presence of diverse Catholic missionaries from the Franciscan, Augustinian, and Capuchin monks, to the Dominican and Jesuit orders, to name the most prominent religious organizations, all working under the aegis of the Portuguese Crown.

The Portuguese were therefore the first Europeans to establish small trading posts along the African coasts so that they could expand their business with the native populations and, consequently, obtain the much-needed goods of gold, salt, minerals, precious metals, and spices, thus bypassing the Venetians and, most of all, the costly but not always reliable Muslim intermediaries of the Maghreb, Egypt, and the Middle East... (Levi 364).

This growth put the Portuguese language at odds with neighboring communities' languages, yet it also allowed the fomenting of a space in which, through commerce, the Portuguese language could find itself within a relationship of tolerance on behalf of its new neighbors. One may in fact recognize the place of the aforementioned missionaries in breaking through the barriers which could have, in the pre-independence period, placed a greater strain on colonial and local relationships. These co-colonizers (alongside their military and governmental colleagues) achieved an admirable stability and peace, relatively speaking, through the keeping of written records of local and regional languages and "sociolinguistic features" of those languages during the process of conversion of local populations to Christianity (365-66). This appreciation shown toward the cultures and languages of the colonized peoples in the interior is most likely one of the principle characteristics of Portuguese colonialism which no doubt kept the situation from worsening into intolerance, or even less desirable, open conflict. Language use in such a context, on the other hand, tended toward limiting itself to grammars and other texts in Portuguese and one other language – in the case of Angola, this language was usually Kimbundu (381-82).

By the middle of the 20th Century the once solely Lusitanian language had, on the one hand, become synonymous with the European (in this case, Portuguese) colonizer, and on the other, it had also become the most widely spoken language in the colony. Portuguese had grown to an imposed acceptance as the language of instruction in schools in both the major cities and in the countryside as early on as the 1920s, when power was consolidated by the Portuguese catholic / Salazarist state and the language of the colonizing nation applied universally (Kandjimbo, "A Dimensão," 59-61). (Education was, of course, a very limited commodity in the Portuguese colonies, as evidenced in previous scholarship from

Arenas, Chabal, and Kandjimbo). Yet, it should be emphasized that the language remained limitedly a língua franca, albeit a well-disseminated one, only until the years approaching the end of the War of Independence, in the early 1970s. According to António Jacinto in an interview, Portuguese and other languages (in this case, Kimbundu) were widely spoken, with a predominance of the Portuguese language for intercultural communication and for work within the colonial bureaucracy, even in the 1930s:

> Naquela época era obrigatório para os colonos, para os empregados dos colonos e para os funcionários saberem falar quimbundo, naquela região, como o tinha sido noutras ... No Golungo, sim, havia escola, já a fronteira era um bocado mais acentuada – teria um lado onde se falava só português, outro onde se falava só quimbundo. Mas mesmos assim, na zona, o português era muito cultivado. Havia uma tradição ali de uma burguesia nacional, que estudava – que tinha ido estudar até em Portugal –, com um culto pelas letras, também um culto pelo direito, porque era uma zona de conflito pela posse das terras e havia sempre envolvimento judicial ... . (Laban 163)

(Eng, "In that era it was obligatory for the colonists, for their employees, and for the burocrats to know how to speak Kimbundu, in that region, as it had been in others ... In Golungo, certainly, there was a school, right at the border it was a bit more accentuated – there would be one side where only Portuguese was spoken, other where only Kimbundu was spoken. Yet, despite this, Portuguese was very much upheld in the region. There was a tradition there of national bourgeois, who would study – who had even gone to study in Portugal –, with a worship of literature, also a cult of the law, because it was a region of conflict for the possession of territory and there was always judicial involvement.")

If one is to accept Jacinto's narrative as a perspective on the true linguistic situation in pre-war Angola, then it would also be illogical to assume that Portuguese, by this time, was a language spoken only in the larger cities.[44] It seems, in this case and according to previously noted scholarship on the topic, that the spread of Portuguese in Angola would have begun based on the spread of colonial and ecumenical rule-of-law outside of the cities as much as it had been implanted firmly within the cities. This would give the Portuguese language a strong basis in the general population as a lingua franca and would also help to settle the language's roots deeper into multiple social arenas in the country.

The 1960s saw a shift in population which would have a direct effect on language use in the country. It was at this point that the refugees from other areas of the country began pouring into the cities, and particularly into Luanda, as the forces embattled in the rural areas felt no remorse about laying waste to vast areas of these regions and decimating the relatively undefended population (Birmingham 159). By the end of the war in 1975, the MPLA-controlled government, whose majority either spoke only Portuguese or simply ignored the other language(s) around which some of the party's leaders had been raised, began to construct a national government using personnel who spoke fluent Portuguese (Birmingham 158). The process of linguistic and cultural consolidation on the part of the most powerful armed group in the new country, along with the aforementioned spread of Portuguese over the century or so beforehand and the massive movements of people from the rural to the urban regions (Severo 23-24) would have had the effect, over the relatively short period of two decades, of de-incentivizing the use of other languages in favor of Portuguese and subsequently "nativizar" (Eng.: "nativizing") what had been in most areas of Angola a well-known, but certainly not ingrained, European language (Matta, *Literatura*, 32), as it were. One may then conclude that, unlike most other countries in sub-Saharan Africa, Angola as a linguistic phenomenon may come to find an explanation for its uniqueness through historical, religious, political, and military means.

---

[44] This is evidenced in many parts of Sub-Saharan African from this study's discussion in reference to the former colonizer's languages of Anglophone and Francophone Africa.

Chabal comments critically on the Angolan government's attempts and creating a palpable national identity both during and after the Angolan Civil War when he states that "the nationalists remained bitterly disunited until independence [which had] ushered in a period of civil conflict...the war may make less explicit the failure of the Angolan regime's blueprint for the construction of the nation" due to the desire for a pluralistic system of governance by the populace while facing the thinly-veiled Marxist dictatorship in charge (57). (It would be of interest to note that the "civil conflict" to which Chabal refers ended shortly before the publication of his text.) This duality, the populace-centered ideal versus the stark reality of a single-party regime which pervades the period and continues to today, may help to explain the disempowerment of cultures not aligned with the new government (and in particular, those whose political leanings were not in support of the MPLA). When taken jointly with the aforementioned unique linguistic situation of the country, particularly in the larger, urban areas, the fundamental reasons for the Portuguese language's rapid spread throughout Angola become clear.

As such, here it will be possible to trace more closely the sociopolitical underpinnings of the pre-independence period social and literary matrix, its utopian discourse in the midst of a very conflictive rebellion, and the manner by which the poetic reflects on the use of language as an essential tool for that discourse. It is recommended, then, to begin with a brief discussion of the political history of pre-independence. (Note 1)

During the period leading up to Angolan independence, three principle rebel groups had formed based on the older geopolitical divisions of the colony: the MPLA ("Movimento Popular de Libertação de Angola") (Eng., "The Popular Liberation Movement of Angola"), UNITA ("União Nacional para a Independência Total de Angola") (Eng., "The National Union for the Total Independence of Angola"), and the FNLA ("Frente Nacional de Libertação de Angola") (Eng., "Angolan National Liberation Front"). Each had begun to create a unique political discourse which indicated both a sociopolitical trajectory and a measurable level of antagonism in contrast to the other two. While the

MPLA adopted the discourse of communism, the other two took a more nominal political standing toward liberation from the Portuguese. Each also found differing sets of external supporting organizations and governments (these included South Africa, Cuba, and the United States, among others), yet another element which aided in fomenting a lasting division between the parties (Birmingham 146-51).[45]

Within the discourse of each lies a fundamental approach to language which, although not spoken within the discourse itself, is essential to it. This is the notion of "unity in diversity," one so essential it is often referred to in political speeches by various members of the upper echelons of the Angolan government.[46] Yet, it always appears expressed through the lens of the only language capable of transcending the limitations of the country's linguistic diversity, and thus, supposed incomprehensibility. That language, given the cultural and geographical variety of origins among members of each rebel groups and their respective leadership, would have to be Portuguese. Every member of each party's elite not only spoke the language, many had either abandoned the traditional language of his people or had never spoken it to begin with, at least with any amount of measurable fluency (as is the case with António Jacinto, whose parentage originated in Portugal). Alongside this historical truth is the position which the language had held in each liberation movement, in order to preserve the same spirit of unity and comprehensibility between members. As peoples from various localities in Angola (from differing cultural and linguistic backgrounds) joined in the struggle against the Portuguese colonial government, the need for a unified source of communication had become necessary.[47] This form,

---

[45] It may be emphasized that the rapid transition from a democratic ideal to a single-party state occurred in a similar way in Angola as it had throughout the rest of Sub-Saharan Africa in the 1970s (Chabal, *A History*, 51).

[46] One excellent example from even more recent times appears in the published transcription of a speech on civility in Angola, given by Roberto de Almeida, Vice-Chairperson of the MPLA in 2010, and shows as a reference to a core belief of the MPLA since its inception (par. 1).

[47] Although each party was rooted in a different area of the country (Udogu 80), enough

again, would have to be Portuguese, the most obvious choice given the longevity of Portuguese colonialism in Angola, the language's expansion into the interior, and more recent adoption within social strata not directly related to a limited bureaucracy.

Parting from the phenomenon mentioned above, this need arose quickly and, due to the probability of it having been coupled with the ire the Angolan people felt toward the Portuguese during this period, would have underscored the base contradiction of the nation's linguistic state. No one regional language could become the primary, national one without marginalizing a significant portion of the country's population; yet, the language of the colonizer brought with it a reticence toward the language's use.

It is, in fact, by way of the poetic that one may observe this process within a revolutionary, pre-independence context, and judge it to be reasonable accordingly:

> Poetry was the most appropriate revendicatory [sic] medium both because it was plastic enough to encompass a form of expression which undermined the colonial legitimating discourse and because it was supremely apt at linking the poetic 'I' with the collective re-appropriation of the African 'We'. Poetry enabled the colonized both to express his rejection of assimilation and to construct the cultural foundations of a new nationality. (Chabal, "Aspects," 33)

The link between the individual self and the national self did indeed find this link within a poetic discourse.[48] This new nationality

---

overlap occurred so as to make the notion of three separate groups with three separate languages an untenable one (Birmingham 148-50).

[48] Chabal's theory of the bifurcated poetic voice, in the present context and without taking into account the perceived need for linguistic unity, would indicate that the politically aligned poets of the era recognized this plasticity all too well.

would, nonetheless, have to be built upon a common foundation; one of the most influential elements of that foundation would be what had transformed from a language of the five-century prolonged European colonizer into the only possible common language for the country.[49]

One may note in the poetry of the period the attempt to create an independent, post-colonial space for Angolan national identity outside of the outright rebellion of Agostinho Neto but expressing also a need for nation building even before the war for independence had ended. The beginning of a re-construction of Angolan identity through the poetry of Neto, as much as through the inspiring yet also telling words of António Jacinto, becomes obvious.[50] Each author's use of the Portuguese language and explicit presentation of regional languages and cultural practices is much more prevalent in the former; the latter will reveal a preference toward national unity both metaphorically and linguistically, although he

---

[49] Before moving toward an analysis of specific poetic examples linked both by personal and by spatial / temporal circumstance, it is wise to mention the period's prose. Both the work itself and its subsequent dissemination, as Arenas has indicated, reflect the singular and utopian ideals expressed in political narratives from the point of view of the urbanized class:

> Literary journals and magazines became an important vehicle to disseminate knowledge about the various Portuguese African colonies among well-education Africans based either in the metropolis or on the African continent. There were a number of publications … circulated among the lettered elites. (*Lusophone*, 162).

Although the ideals of communication seemed destined for all, only those from the "assimilados," or socially assimilated, Angolan social classes (those who, once established as the ruling cadre of the MPLA's hierarchy, would take power in the country as higher level elected or appointed officials of the government) would have access to it. This contradiction would have two main effects: it would later spill out into the conflict between the (linguistically) unifying tendencies of the urban populations and the rural ones, and it would force the spread of the language beyond the urban regions of Luanda and Benguela as the Portuguese language would prove its vital role in offering opportunities to Angolans not of the empowered classes. Tavares' poetry will give some indication of this eventual tension; Kandjimbo's will make more explicit its apparent consequences, albeit in a very diplomatic sense.

[50] I will recontextualize this statement later within and outside of the Lusophone space in the poetry of Luís Kandjimbo and its rich, mimetic criticism.

does not explicitly use any other language but Portuguese to do so.⁵¹ One may then classify this poetic tendency as representative of the moment of a focus on unification in Angolan poetry, within the context of language's use within the nation-building project as each writer has understood it.

Again, it must be emphasized that the notion of identity as expressed through such an epistemology had served the first stages of this project, or those of creating a space for the agglomeration of various regions of the territory into a single nation. This period will, vis-à-vis the present interpretation, constitute the basis of the "first phase" of Angolan poetic expression, according to the socio-linguistic and socio-literary framework established in this study. To the detriment of those regions and their diverse peoples and cultures, such a project has also had the ill-desired but not altogether unexpected consequence of the acceptance of the new government whose cultural, linguistic, and political practices (and eventually commercial and other ties) to the old colonial regime, despite official criticism of that regime, would reveal themselves more clearly as time went on.⁵²

After the colonial wars and the establishment of the MPLA in the 1970s as the major political power in the country, "language was power in postcolonial African politics and it was the *assimilados* who spoke Portuguese, the language of command" (Birmingham 149). These *assimilados* had taken part in the colonial government and had become a part of Portuguese colonial culture. The party used their knowledge of the Portuguese language as a method of maintaining their foothold on the

---

[51] In this critical framework I will view Jacinto's work as more a philosophical statement than as a blatantly epistemological one. In doing so, such a poetic performance will highlight the need to codify the poetic and the linguistic as parts of the new nation's sociocultural matrix, or as Matta states, "no sistema nacional" (*Literatura*, 36) (Eng., "in the national system").

[52] It would also be of importance to note that Chabal, in his introduction to the 1996 volume titled *The Postcolonial Literature of Lusophone Africa* states that, while the European languages spoken in Africa are not «native» to the region, they become important in establishing communication with the world as well as becoming part of the nation-building apparatus (5-6).

country throughout the 1980s, since this had been the language of colonial government and the only single unifying one in the country (157). The new elite of the country, by the turn of the 21st Century, behaved in ways all too similar to the colonial government of the 1950s and 60s (184). On the surface this mirrors the process of language assimilation in other, non-Lusophone African countries. However, it becomes clear that the use of Portuguese grew as a response by incoming Angolans who had fled the country decades before, as well as by those displaced internally during the colonial wars.

The final decades of the Twentieth Century and beginning of the Twenty First have been marked by prolonged periods of civil conflict and war, a peace made by the total defeat of one of the three major parties that had survived the war of independence, and the consolidation of the country's government by the aforementioned MPLA, the party led by Agostinho Neto.[53] The promises of peace and unity that this new government under Neto's presidency has made proved untenable, aiding only in a conflagration of the strife which continuously gripped Angola. This brought the regions under the MPLA's control, whether already in that condition upon the independence war's end or later on, under heavy scrutiny, cementing further the party's hold on an ever-larger portion of the general populace.

The factious nature of the anticolonial forces in the war, "each with its own range of supporters, weapons, and ideological visions" (Birmingham 141), continued into the independence era with a civil war which devastated and subjugated even further the Angolan countryside and its peoples. When compounded by the Portuguese's ability to play each faction against the other during the war of independence (Chabal 16), the notion of collaboration between the three (and later on only two) parties in the post-independence period became that much more unlikely.

---

[53] Chabal (10) speaks of a "three-party" civil war; given the relative predominance of UNITA and the MPLA in the conflict (and the FLNA's relative weakness against the former two), and the unilateral results of the war, one may also choose to interpret the Angolan Civil War as one of primarily two larger parties.

With the return of Angolan families from Europe and the consolidation of the creole-led government in Luanda in the 1980s (Birmingham 157-59), the MPLA consolidation of the country was assured despite the on-going civil war(s) outside of the capital. As time passed, the hope of forming a communist-based nation became impossible. It seems due to this lost ideal that the conversion from a "Marxist-Leninist" evolution toward a capitalist one was realized, despite the continued discourse of the former on the part of the MPLA. With the fall of the Soviet Block the veil of the former gave way completely to the latter (Arenas, *Lusophone*, 164). Of course, this change, while allowing the MPLA to continue to hold onto the power which the various civil conflicts of the period had allowed the party to accumulate, did not aid the party's government in Luanda in assuring trust among the country's citizenry. As an unfortunate consequence to such a troubled, halted, and failed evolution toward true nationhood, this situation has come to form the structural and philosophical basis of the regime that exists today, even after the civil war's end in 2002.[54]

One of the more prevalent aspects of the regime has been its discourse of political and cultural unification and utopia, despite the evidence to the contrary. Writers have been quick to criticize this as malicious and false advertising on the part of Angola's government. "The heavy utopian investment by writers in the creation of a free and just society …, even among those writers who served in government positions, has receded in favor of a multiplicity of cultural, sociocultural, and historical concerns…" (Arenas, *Lusophone*, 165). As previously discussed, in the literary community [primarily disseminated through the União de Escritores Angolanos (Eng., "Union of Angolan Writers"), an organization established by the MPLA-led government shortly after independence (Leite 153-54)] the prose writers of this period

---

[54] It should be noted that, while I may treat the period of 1974 to 2002 as one long civil conflict punctuated by periods of relative stability, historians such as Chabal and Birmingham have divided the period into various, shorter conflicts. The "Civil War" as Birmingham describes it (173) began after the elections of 1992, ended in 1993, then began again in 1998 (178-79), for example.

have focused on the disenchantment of Angola's social and political realities versus the rather "utopian" discourse of its government (*Lusophone*, 160). It is during this time that Angola has seen the real postcolonial, multicultural, and multifaceted nature of the consequences of a reductive epistemology of unity within a paradigmatic context of the nationhood ideal as forced upon a diverse populace, in contrast to the relatively simpler and much more positive message offered to readers during the previous historical and literary period (by way of works written during the "first phase" of Contemporary Angolan poetry). Such a process has, in essence, attempted to remove the same diversity which the previous period's writings had exalted, replacing it with a false dichotomy. As Ana Paula Tavares stated in an interview in 2007:

> [i]mmediately after independence, there was a scramble to fix a mythology that could reference us as Angolans. At that time, the classic psychological tactics of nations killing their cultural fathers and mothers, and of including some people while excluding others, were rife. (Ribeiro 148-9)

The virtual enslavement of rural workers in cities such as Luanda and Benguela during the revolutionary period by the American and other European contract companies (run by the Portuguese as local contract managers) did not aid in alleviating the situation (Birmingham 138-9). It is logical to see that, in order to survive under such conditions, the workers needed a very strong grasp of the Portuguese language and could see the need for such knowledge.[55] In other words, to state that the creation of an Angolan national identity has been performed in a socially responsible way is not the most justifiable of conclusions; to ignore the fact of the language's adoption by a much larger portion of the populace, whether for reasons of nationalism or pure survival, and the fact of its existence as a native language of the majority of that populace, is also not justifiable.

---

[55] It has been said that Angolans "... growing up in [the musseques] were very quickly deprived of their own heritage to such an extent that many predominant writers including Agostinho Neto and Mário António do not speak ... Kimbundu" (Burness, *Fire*, xiv).

It should at this point be emphasized that the purpose of this study is not to *defend* state-based national identity building, but rather to *reveal* (by way of the poetry written during and after the establishment of the Angolan state) how voices from within the accepted literary canon outline both its strengths and its potential (if not palpable) pitfalls. Among these one may include such issues the culture of class distinctions based on urban vs. rural and various other factors created during the colonial period which have remained to this day (Chabal, *A History*, 109-10).

The notion of hybridity, when added to this matrix, has become invaluable in offering a nuanced understanding of Angolan poetry and the Portuguese language's place in it. As Sousa Santos has argued, the birth of the so-called "Prospero" and "Caliban" in a single being has happened very concretely in Lusophone Africa ("Between Prospero and Caliban," 13-14). The formation of an individual or set of individuals who espouse aspects of both the colonizer and the colonized, in many cases at the same time, may become a group which creates, rather than one that follows or dominates. Particularly in the present case of Angola and of the poetic trends prevalent in this contemporary space, a reading of the poetic voice as part of that hybridized, empowered and simultaneously devalued, discourse will reveal the construction of an identity unlike those of the peoples residing in neighboring nations and nation-states. One may observe this phenomenon via a careful readings of poems by Ana Paula Tavares and Luís Kandjimbo (for reasons specific to their thematic development, differing social standings within Angolan society, and focus on intracultural and intralinguistic topics), although texts by other authors (both contemporary to these and their antecedents) may also be possible.

It has been shown this division as symptom of a greater divide, that of two general literary "pillars." One of these looks to be a literature "anchored in oral tradition," one more closely aligned with the expression of a less Europeanized Angola. The other seems, although not necessarily in contrast to the former, "relevant to … anti-colonial ambitions" within the search for a notion of "*Angolanidade*" in their writing (Chabal, "Aspects," 19). This means that, instead of looking through the lens of intimacy versus national historicity, there exists the notion that poetry either looks toward the pre-Portuguese period cultures (or at least what may remain of them, as time passes) or toward the synchronic context and in open opposition to Portuguese colonialism. Such an excision of the political from the historical does not necessarily stem from a desire to remove all ties between the politicized and assumedly less powerful cultures (those not borne from the urban, mostly Portuguese-speaking populations of Luanda and Benguela) of the country. Rather, in this sense one may perceive the emphasis on the social, either in a diachronic appreciation for the country's cultural heterogeneity or on a synchronic one, focusing entirely on more recent events and their sociopolitical consequences.[56]

Such will be the case, as this study will argue, in the poetics of late 20th and early 21st Century Angolan poetry there is relatively little loss of the poet's / the poetic's tendency toward orality in poetry, even when the subject matter tends more toward the anti-colonial (or the discourse of disillusionment more common in the post-colonial period). The multiple foci of the diachronic, within the context of social and political evolution, and of the synchronic, with its open criticism of the cultural and linguistic rush toward disaster which will define Angolan history from 1974 to 2002, converge both to glorify the new nation's place within its own utopian approximation to self-actualization, and later, to rebuild its self-image after the decades of war and decimation which befell the country during the final decades of the 20th Century and early 21st Century.[57]

---

[56] I should note that, according to Chabal's article, both Vieira and Neto utilize tendencies from oral literature in speaking of issues in the context of the independence movement of the 1950s and 60s.

[57] Secco adds that "[i]n much of the poetry produced by members of the most recent Angolan generations,

dreams are found enveloped in a crepuscular vision." ("Postcolonial," 124). The implications of this perspective stem from a sharp differentiation in the overall poetic thematic in Angola which this study means to explore further in the discussion of Neto's and Kandjimbo's respective works.

Within the more politically charged tendency as Chabal has described in any case authors such as Agostinho Neto, António Jacinto (both of whose work will be analyzed in greater detail in the next chapter), Fonseca Wochay, and José Luandino Vieira (although not a poet, Vieira's work sets the tone for the heteroglossia which will characterize the Angolan Portuguese dialects and upon which the modern use of the language and concomitant power structures are based) become even more visible.[58] On the latter, one may find the poetry of Ana Paula Tavares, Luís Kandjimbo (whose poems will appear in a more focused study in Chapter IV), and Manuel Rui. As evidenced by the dates during which these authors published their works, one may assume that, under this theory, the process of differentiation is not one of evolution from one state to another in the period under consideration (1950 to the present); rather, it should appear to be one of a synchronic process of varied foci based on a previous and subtle bifurcation of essentially the same tendency.

It is in this sense, and with a vision toward a more complex and descriptive theoretical model of this very complex literary process, that one may then view this epistemology as yet another convergence. The alternative reading proposed in this study will stem from the intersection of Chabal's epistemological division of the essential split in post-structuralist critical theory between Derridean synchronic orientation toward "différance," or the moment of play based on the oppositions between and within differing ideals (Olson 248), and Foucault's general theories on "historicism" and its foundation within a diachronically focused perspective (Bell 297-300), in view of Angolan poetic evolution, and with Matta's notions alongside of the simultaneous "epic" versus "constructive" trajectories which Angolan poetry seems to have taken.[59]

---

[58] It should also be noted that the União de Escritores Angolanos ("Angolan Writers Union"), primary publisher for most poets in Angola, actually is part of the central government even though it has tended to stand apart from government discourse beginning in the 1990s (Laban 906).

[59] This recombination of the purely theoretical with the notably contextual aspects of Angolan poetry and poetic discourse should resemble both Dali's statements concerning

These assertions and their potential visibility to the reader will reside within a deeper thematic and contextual analysis of poetic works by Neto and Jacinto (from what will be known here as the first "phase" of this poetic discourse), and then in those by Tavares and Kandjimbo (corresponding to the second "phase"). I will not delve into their verses here; rather, below I will illustrate the examples from the remaining writers of those enumerated above (Vieira, Wochay, and Rui) to exemplify, in general terms, the artistic tendencies of the two periods in question. The presence of cultural and linguistic combination and / or stratification as delineated thus far will also play a primary role in the description of such examples, setting the stage insofar as may be necessary and appropriate for the greater study of the poetic reflection on the complexities of language use and apparent linguistic-cultural appropriation in Angola in the chapters to come.

José Luandino Vieira was a writer of European parentage, although distinctly Angolan in self-identification (Chabal, "Aspects," 20). In Arenas' discussion the poet's biography one may find the first notable case of a recombination of the local lexicon (mostly from Kimbundu, as the protagonists of his writings came largely from either the Luanda "musseques" or other urban areas) within the Portuguese language (*Lusophone*, 163).[60] Although this deliberately bilateral lexical and grammatical exchange did not serve as an explicit commentary on the political order, Vieira's creativity in placing a new linguistic form within Portuguese has given a voice to what, even several decades ago, was a nascent yet very distinctive dialect of Portuguese.[61]

---

the need for a dual focus on form as much as on context as well as Ahluwalia's critical judgments regarding the peril of non-contextualized literary analysis, from this study's introduction.

[60] It is curious that Xitu, a contemporary of Vieira's, has been recorded as criticizing his use of Kimbundu in his Portuguese texts as words of one who "não sabe falar bem" (Laban 128) ("does not know how to speak well") the language, and as such, making rather artificial his use of it. Xitu then continues making clear that Angolans have a preference to speak Portuguese, even though in more emotional states they may revert to isolated words in Kimbundu or "quimbundualizado" (129) ("Kimbundualized") – noting the insertion of the term "dual" intralexically ("quimbundo+dual+izado") for ironic effect.

Furthermore, and beyond the exaltation of an emerging new dialect, Vieira's work also represents a socially compromised criticism focusing particularly on white settlements and aftermath of colonization (Ornelas 198). His work moves, then, beyond the discourse of the colonized African self into the realm of the Africanized self, similar to that which Knopfli achieves in the poem discussed previously. In this manner, and due to his very social focus, his prose will qualify as pertaining to what Matta had referred to as "epic" literature, under the specifications given, for his place in expressing and meditating on the hopes of what he views as a nation in peril.

I will emphasize again that Vieira's narrative voice(s) also reveal(s) a linguistic combination with Kimbundu which seems to move beyond simple lexical choices. This is not solely a ubiquitous way of reflecting on language in a neo-realist fashion (as the reader will see in the case of Agostinho Neto's poetry). Rather, it is viewed as a literary moment of national Angolan identity creation through language (Dali 290-91).[62] His work, in this sense, represents (and one could argue, exemplifies) the creation of a codified Angolan Portuguese (Chabal, "Aspects," 29-30) which would influence greatly the poetry of the period and would come to found the notion of an essentially and ontologically validated Angolan self-expression in Portuguese language.

While Vieira's prose represents an initial moment of national conscience and as a major voice within the Angolan literary canon, works by the poet Fonseca Wochay (1949) stand as both a model of socially-oriented poetry and as somewhat of an enigma in the Angolan poetic

---

[61] Other analyses have yielded strikingly different results. In his seminal work on Angolan literature, Hamilton, for example, views this as more of a "smattering" of linguistic anomalies meant more to show intercultural richness through an invented language than as a reflection of real-life speech (*Voices*, 134-36).

[62] In linguistic terms, Vieira's prose represents a moment in which the natural "code-mixing" and "borrowing" between the "dominant and a minority language" (in this case, between Portuguese and Kimbundu) (Batibo 28-9) may find its literary expression.

world. Little is known of the writer's work, except that he not only writes as a poet but has appeared also as a journalist.

Wochay's poetic discourse is evidently one of direct confrontation with the violence of Portuguese colonialism during the independence period. It speaks to the violence perpetrated against the Angolan people and the immediate consequences of decolonization on the Angolan people and psyche in the 1970s and early 1980s.

His verses tend to speak very directly to the issues of social struggles, without losing sight of the orality of traditional poetry. The combination remits to Chabal's notion of a compromised poetic as well as to Matta's idea of the "epic" Angolan verse. Poems such as the excerpt from "Viver é Lutar" ("To Live and To Fight"), from his book *Poesia de Combate* (1974) and re-published separately in 1982, may serve to highlight his works' courageous thematic:

Viver é Lutar:

Bater,

bater no milho

bater na massambala

bater na batata doce

bater ao algodão

bater para a defesa das crianças

bater pelo amanhã das mulheres

bater em todo o mundo que esmaga.

To *A Nação*, with Love

Lutar,

...

(Marques 324)

(Eng.,

"To mash

to mash the corn

to mash the sorghum

to mash the sweet potato

to mash up the cotton

to mash in defense of the children

to mash for women's tomorrow

to mash the world that tyrannizes

To struggle

...")

    The poem is evidently part of an overtly politicized, anticolonial voice. It combines elements of Angolan culture, particularly the practice of hand-mashing ("bater") the various staple foods, and combined language use, as is evidenced in the example below, to outline independence and unity through a unique identity. "Massambala," in particular, is the Angolan word for sorghum (in standard European Portuguese it is called "sorgo;" in Brazil, "milho-zaburro"). The poem's repetitive structure, consistent use of anaphor and parallelisms, and its emphatic, rhetorical qualities – the verb "bater" can also mean "to hit" or "to strike" with force – serve to illustrate the thematic elements mentioned above.

In the works of each writer seen above, a very specific set of themes and linguistic structures appear, namely, those of social injustice and the desire for freedom (either from the colonial master or from the aftermath of colonialism). There is also, although not explicitly treated in the works, a culturally-appropriate usage of the former colonizer's language. If viewed as a theme of these works, it may be found expressing a language which has appropriated elements of another one so as to remain a viable and primary means of communication, as is the case in Vieira's work, or as the primary means of the call to rebellion, as in that of Wochay.[63]

As stated earlier, another poetic trajectory does exist. This one concentrates its focus as much on the political as it does on the personal aspects of the Angolan people's rise to nationhood and their subsequent disenchantment with the falsehoods the new nation's government has propagated. The example below illustrates this poetic strain.

Manuel Rui represents, par excellence, the more subtle and intimate "constructive" variant of Angolan poetry, according to the model presented above (although never losing sight of his political leanings, a point which must remain clear despite the tendencies visible in any one writer's artistic praxis). An activist against colonialism and government abuses, his pre and post-independence artistic works outline utopian hopes and discourse followed by the disillusionment (Arenas, "Manuel Rui," 160) of post-independence. Striking are Rui's use of Angolan Portuguese terms in his prose (161-62) and the development, over time, of works which focus more on individual struggles within the new

---

[63] The next chapter highlights Neto's poetry and remits to this "epic" poetic strain in formal and symbolic terms, although his use of language in the vein reminiscent of Vieira will undoubtedly reflect a greater process of the construction of a power structure in the nascent country.

context, one which includes the sharp division between the relatively prosperous urban social classes and the underdeveloped interior (162) (as opposed to a much more and almost purely socially-oriented one as seen in the former case). In his poetry, such as the case of the collection titled *11 Poemas em Novembro*, as in many of his other works, "a Angolaneidade política e cultural" (Mendes 99) appears evidenced.

In focusing on Rui's poems one may find examples of such a "constructive" poetic, or one which builds on the more intimate and individual, sentimental nature of the human condition to create a new space for a national identity. The well-known poem below, written during the first years of independence, may shed some light on the duality present in his verses:

"Manhã de Onze de Novembro" (leitura terceira)

Ouvir o mar

por detrás do cheiro a maresia

e ver teu rosto

na ondulação tão breve

doar esta manhã de fantasia

a um quissanje mais leve

para um vento do fogo

dedilhar

Içar nos braços

a manhã primeira

correr à procura de lugar

da frente no comício

para pôr bandeira

roer unhas do sol

saber acreditar

que esta manhã sem ti

é verdadeira.

(Rui 19)

(Eng:

"Morning of November 11th (third reading)

To hear the sea

behind the scent of sea air

and to see your face

in the waves such brief

pain this morning of fantasy

to the lighter *quissange*

strumming

to a burning wind

To hoist in your arms

the first morning

to run in search of a place

at the front of the rally

to place the flag

to bite the sun's nails

knowing to believe

that this morning without you

is real.")

      Rui's poem is also a call to rally in the name of this new, Angolan nation. Although it does not call out to the people in the same, almost bellicose manner as that of Wochay, the presence of national unity in the face of challenge does not escape us; one also do not lose sight of a more intimate focus within the poem. Here, in fact, the reader may find both the political struggle for nation and the individual's pain from the other's absence as simultaneous forces functioning in a subtle yet palpably dolorous harmony. The poem, as such, reveals both a social and an intimate focus – the individual suffers as the homeland struggles. The matching of these forces in the poem aid it in adhering to the notion of a "constructive" poetic as described above, in confluence with (although not at all in the same social vein as) the less intimate and overtly more socially-oriented "epic" type.

However, it is not advisable to gaze upon Angolan poetics with such a simplified system – other elements continue working within and outside the poem. The "força desmitificadora" (Matta, *Literatura*, 83) (Eng., "demystifying force") of literature in the 1980s also becomes apparent in the particular images of the poem, such as the counterpoint of placing the flag and biting "the sun's nails." The poetic voice seems constructive yet also critical, as noted in the general characteristics of poetry in late 1970s and early 1980s Angola (82).

With this perspective in mind one may view an alternate framework from which to approach the analysis of both the political and the cultural aspects of this contemporary Angolan poetic expression. This framework will take advantage of the spirit of the models presented above while also taking into account the possibly contradictory complexities of the poems each astutely attempt to classify. It will also be feasible in this way to create a space in which the rapid change from one thematic to another may fall alongside the differing approaches to the purpose of poetry on which former theories have been based.

In other words, beyond the divided approximations these poets reflect there is another manner by which to organize these and other authors' works into an evolutionary (albeit rapid), rather than synchronic (or series of synchronic), process(es). This will be similar to the argument Chabal presents, although occurring in a temporal context rather than simply a spatial one; this context happens with the change from pre- to post-independence, in a period of fewer than five years. Given the history of the Portuguese language in Angola as discussed in the previous chapter and its evident adoption by the elite classes of contemporary Angolan society during the 20th Century,[64] alongside its incorporation by a relatively

---

[64] I will be referring to Arenas and Birmingham's works in Chapters III and IV regarding this process of colonial acculturation by the Angolan elites, and then later on by the new

large portion of the general population (again, as compared with the use of European languages in neighboring countries and, in fact, as compared with those languages' use in the majority of Sub-Saharan African countries), it is not only possible but perhaps even preferable to combine the epistemology of the socially compromised poetic as both independent and as present in the more intimate poetic voice as evidenced above with these other, non-artistic forces – the linguistic forces at work in particular. This will allow the designation of an alternative approach to Angolan poetry of the independence and post-independence periods with a focus on language use as a *primary* element of poetic expressive discourse in a social context, rather than as merely a secondary literary or rhetorical technique for prosaic or poetic expression.

In this new vision, or perhaps better said, this revised approximation, the presence of the Portuguese language from the period of c.1950 to the present (the first two decades of the 21st Century) in the context of a nation-building process in Angola as viewed through poetry has undergone two distinctive phases. (Note 2) The process will be similar to the utopian / dystopian evolution of poetry in Anglophone and Francophone contexts in Africa; the linguistic development of Angola, and this development's consequences, will form the cornerstone of the extensive differences to be studied shortly. The most distinctive element of this process will consist of a rapid transitional period, not consistent with the perspectives presented above or in the descriptions of other post-colonial African experiences (namely those of the Anglophone or Francophone Worlds). This will coincide with the concomitantly rapid failure of the MPLA to produce the utopian peace and national unity promised during the final years of the conflict with the Portuguese, a phenomenon to study more closely in the next chapter.

In the "first phase" the language is placed concomitantly with other languages and / or traditions "native" to Angola in a poetic discourse of utopia through which the reader may view an attempt at

---

governing class made up essentially (as I have shown here) of the same individuals.

creating a sort of politically convenient unity through diversity. (Note 3) Such modes of expression provide the Portuguese language as both one of many forms of communication and as the most useful and unifying mode of conveying a national discourse. As seen in previous scholarship, "... a nacionalização literária precede a independência política ..." (Matta, *Literatura*, 20) (Eng., ".... literary nationalization precedes political independence ..."). Through building a national language and using literature to do so, the leaders of what would eventually become the governing party of the country, in essence, nationalize Portuguese as part of a larger institution which, through other social and historical processes, becomes the majority language. One will observe this process revealed through poems by Agostinho Neto and António Jacinto, two principle figures of the independence period whose poetic voices concretize the discourse of the national through the linguistic universality of Portuguese, the language through which all others are seemingly understood.

The "second phase" of poetry, in reference to this new reflection on the Portuguese language's use through poetry as a tool for nation-building, occurs principally during the 1980s and continuing to the present in Angola, is that of its own deconstruction. The marginalized self as part of the unsuccessfully integrated national identity becomes paramount to a new, national poetic voice in its sociocultural and artistic function in this phase. Poetry then echoes this reality as revealed through a very quick and immediate change in the tone, theme, and appreciation for linguistic and cultural plurality. The effervescent hope and focus on the future is turned back in on itself, forcing the reader to perceive the underbelly of the official discourse of a singular, national identity. That unity is also broken by way of an open criticism toward language use; rather than celebrating a new, Angolan Portuguese language (one which incorporates all within it in a complex yet harmonious choir), poets utilize the linguistic uniqueness of the true linguistic and cultural issues prevalent in an evolving, postwar Angolan space to argue for a re-evaluation of official views. Such an approximation essentially becomes an argument which attempts to highlight the submission of all other languages and cultures to the one which supports the current MPLA, creole-based government structure. In this phase one also has the opportunity to recognize the possibilities for a pluralistic future which, through their verses, the poets themselves propose (and which stands in opposition to the relative hopelessness of the prose published in the 1990s and beyond as has been and will be noted throughout this study).

In the works of Ana Paula Tavares and Luís Kandjimbo, authors who had supported openly the independence movement and who have lived through the post-independence chaos of Angola from 1975 to 2002, one may view a similar presence of both Portuguese (as the primary language of communication) and other languages / cultural manifestations, not in the same utopian light, but in describing a dystopian sociocultural space, one in which a series of steps has attempted to reduce Angola's linguistic and cultural diversity through reductive and simplifying practices on the part of a government unsupportive of such diversity. The Angolan self, then, does not exist as a united front; the multiplicity of cultures, supposedly a point of pride and of unification for a new postcolonial and free nation, has found itself suppressed linguistically and culturally. This reconfiguration of the poetic space in Angola fits with existing theories on the excision between the utopian discourse of the first period and the aforementioned "força desmitificadora" in the years following independence and leading up to today (Matta, *Literatura*, 83).

Given this new perspective, one must remember that there are two pre-existing methods by which to classify the evolution of an Angolan poetic. One is thematically charged and simultaneous throughout time, that is, it stems from the bifurcation of either the need for a socially-bound poetic, or for that of an intimately rooted voice in relative isolation emotionally from those around it. The other, an epistemological evolution which reveals two distinctive social and artistic epochs, bases its approach on an interpretation of social, linguistic, cultural, literary, and individual / local context, rather than solely on more abstract notions of solidarity versus intimacy. Being that the latter conforms better to the contours poetry takes with regard to language preference and commentary on that preference's sociopolitical bearings, this analysis will most likely seem to the reader to prefer this approximation over the former.

As such, it will be important to distinguish the perspective this book puts forth with that which Inocência Matta, Chabal, Arenas, and others would deem the "utopian" pre-independence and immediate post-independence urban context and the opposing "post-colonial" period, during which discourse moves from the very hopeful to the very disenchanted, a process laid out in many other countries in the contemporary African sociopolitical landscape (Arenas, *Lusophone*, 169). The present study focuses on the use of language as a two-phase process of the evolution of a notion of the former colonizer's language as forming the basis for a new, national language, one which serves as part of a construction toward the unity of the new nation. In its second phase, then, the rapid evolution within the dystopian realities of that language as part and parcel of a simplistic and destructive process of nation building takes center stage. The themes which each poet highlights in his or her poetry, as well as those present within each individual poem, will vary with the more individualized context of each one. The epistemological discourse of each, on the other hand, will reveal these two phases in both a general sense as well as in detail, bringing about an alternate reading and contextualization of several of Angola's canonical poetic voices.

It should be noted that a similar theoretical model to the one I offer here has existed for some time. At least in terms of the diachronic framework on which it depends, Ana Mafalda Leite's chapter (1996) on Angolan literature in this period describes a tripartite and more paused evolutionary process to poetry. Her work states that the independence war generation, or that of the *Mensagem* generation from 1950 to 1970 (142), the writers from the 1970s and 80s (146-47, and those of the 1980s to 1996 (153-57). The first group based its writing on "clear lyrical or dramatic qualities which serve well the purpose of 'recovering' a literature of Angola grounded in oral tradition" (146). The second, in this interpretation, did the same but with a somewhat less "nationalistic" voice and experimental poetic themes and forms (146), although still conserving a perspective on the nation-building process (153). The third and most recent (at least at the time of the study's publication) was, as Leite puts it, "in (dis)continuity with the poetry of the *Mensagem* generation and of the generation of the 1970s" (164) due to its goal of "formal innovation, intertextual sensitivity, the experimental deconstruction of language and an opening to the world of sensuality" (164).

On the surface, then, it would seem that the theory I propose here would lack any real sense of innovation when reframed using Leite's insightful and descriptive study. However, the perspective I present here and Leite's own conclusions differ in three principle areas. First, while this book takes the implicit or explicit commentary on language use as an axis for the interpretation of the poetic, Leite's study prefers to focus on a notion of the political as it seems to wane over a forty year period. My study will maintain that this is not the case, as I intend to prove shortly. Second, the view presented here and as detailed above represents a notion of schism, not between the political and intimate, but between the politicized use of language and the contextualized and deconstructive re-evaluation of a socially reflective use of language [as opposed to the "experimental deconstruction" which Leite describes (164)]. As such, the notion that the intimate somehow attempts to divorce from the political, particularly in women's writing (160-163), will reveal itself as a conclusion which I do not share. Finally, in the view I present in this study there have been three phases in the development of Angolan poetry between 1960 and the 21st Century. Although one may see differences in the forms used by Neto versus those present in the poetry of David Mestre, for example (147-48), the thematic expressed in the work of these poets does not vary significantly from that of poets such as António Jacinto or Wochay. As such, I argue the inclusion of the poets of the 1970s as reflective of a similar nationalist fervor as those of the decade before. This makes yet more evident the rupture between the creative poetic and a more critical one, in view of the nation-building process in Angola, than presented in previous scholarship.

In essence, in the chapters that follow the poetic oevres engendered vis-à-vis a series of events which exercise a direct influence on the unexpectedly widespread use of the Portuguese language in Angola during the final decades of the 20th Century will take center stage. In this search for self and nation, followed immediately and rather abruptly by this new nation's search for self, the linguistic (in)adequacies of this not entirely acceptable mother tongue will become both apparent and, within the contemporary context of self-reconciliation, evermore questioned.

Chapter III: *Phase One – the Struggle for Self and Nation*

Here as elsewhere, analyses have revealed the emergence of a post-colonial Africa looking to forge its own path, yet utilizing many of the same hegemonic structures which the former colonial "masters" left behind. In the case of the English and French-speaking countries, this has led to a difficult and divisive relationship between the urban elites and the rest of the country. For the Portuguese-speaking countries in Africa, and particularly for Angola, the situation is culturally and linguistically more nuanced and complex. There exists a larger population of Portuguese speakers of African descent in these spaces in contrast to those of countries such as Senegal or Nigeria. This unique development of the ideal of a national identity, in part a natural evolution and in part a forced one, has opened the door to various interpretations of itself as having become such an unexpected occurrence in the region.

With respect to the specific case of Angola's linguistic development, what has been presented may be understood as two principle theories on the country's cultural and literary movements, one based on thematic differences, and the other epistemologically based. In the case of the former, there seems to be a tendency either to exalt or to construct, to look inward from a heroic perspective or from a future-oriented one. In the case of the latter, criticism focusing in this direction seems to inculcate a vision of nation-building as either the result of a community-based struggle against the oppressive colonial yoke, or as one borne from the individual experience which the new country faces in terms of its pre- and post-independence political and social issues.

Although one should find each of these approaches as both decisive in their overall vision and revealing in the topics which bear out as a consequence of a literary analysis based on them, neither critical perspective has taken into account the linguistic situation of the country (in which a large percentage speaks Portuguese either as their sole language of communication or bilingually, as the data has indicated) beyond noting that the Lusophone, in its current state, may be viewed as both an anomaly of post-colonial Africa and as a vestige of the colonial period (Matta, *Literatura*, 20-30). The manner in which Portuguese language has been disseminated, and then matured through a potentially codified process, into its place in the urban and semi-urban regions of the country, and just as importantly, its appearance as part of a linguistic / cultural combination whose nature is anything but random, has allowed for the engendering of another possible approximation to Angola's sociocultural and literary development. Through a treating the linguistic phenomenon of Portuguese language's forced adoption, and then appropriation, by the populace as a principle element of the government-oriented nation building process (rather than as a symptom of it) one may now begin to theorize on the literature written during the pre- and post-independence periods as reflecting a poetic (r)evolution. This stance represents a more evolutionary-minded approach, as opposed one which highlights the poetic in Angola as merely a continuous, parallel series of commentaries, as would seem to be the case from either of the previously explicated critical apparatuses.

Within such a context it is evident that the poetic and the political would merge to form a sort of dichotomy between the textual and the spatial. The two poets studied here in particular, both pertaining to the same independence group (and eventual governing body of the new Angolan state) yet each with their differing approaches to the issues of national identity and "unity through diversity,"[65] may serve to exemplify this "first phase" of the poetic within the framework I have proposed here.

António Agostinho Neto is one of very few Lusophone African writers who not only symbolize nationhood within his country, but stand also as a symbol of that country and her literature outside of the

---

[65] This term, or manifestations of it, are relatively common throughout official and unofficial discourse in Angola. Even texts such as on-line news articles go into great detail defending this ideal as part of the officialized identity of the citizen of the Angolan nation-state (Barbeitos, par 1-2).

homeland (Burness, *Fire*, 19). The son of a Presbyterian minister and the principle voice in the Angolan struggle for liberation against the Portuguese colonial system, Neto began writing poetry in the 1940s before he began studying in Portugal. His writing had always a politically-charged base, although he became less prolific in his writing as his leadership in the political realm became better defined, involved greater risk, and grew more time-intensive (Chabal, "Aspects," 32). During his time at university in Portugal his writing began to reveal his very evident sentiments in favor of Pan-Africanism and of independence from any form of external colonization. This support of what in essence was a nascent independence movement in the Portuguese colonies (among those under the control of other European powers) caused him to be arrested on multiple occasions (Abdala 120). These placed him in a position to garner support and lend his abilities in leadership in academic, literary, and much wider circles:

> [W]hile it is clear that there is in the early poems a strong feeling of disorientation, loneliness, and nostalgia which were evidently associated with the difficulty of settling in Portugal, what is interesting is the connection which Neto already makes between personal anguish and the suffering of the African people. (Chabal, "Aspects," 35)

As is well known, Neto served as one of the founders of the idea of "Vamos Descobrir Angola," or the creation of a national consciousness, during the 1940s; this happened just before his time in Portugal as a student. He would ultimately lead a group of writers and resistance fighters in what would eventually be the creation of the MPLA ("Movimento Popular de Libertação de Angola"), the rebel group which would transform into the strongest political unit in the new Republic.

In his work one may observe clearly the belief that the colonizer could be defeated only through the absolute unity of what Neto saw as a fragmented Angolan population (Kandjimbo, "A Dimensão," 64-65). This perspective on collaboration also, as an essential piece of the nation-building process, included his views on poetry as a function of re-creating an independent, African identity. He and others of his generation drew some ideas from the only independent, Portuguese-speaking country to that point, Brazil. "The tone of this early poetry was, naturally enough, one of exhortation in which the poets, often inspired by the modernist Brazilian writers, called on their Angolan colleagues to create a new Angolan literature" (Chabal, "Aspects," 34).[66] His work in the 1940s in founding the Casa dos Estudantes do Império and in fomenting a feeling of "Black Consciousness" among his peers (35-36), beyond his aforementioned poetic and other writings, distinguished him as a man who spoke on behalf of the Portuguese Empire's overseas citizens who desired to shed that citizenship in recognition of their own national aspirations.

His poetry had always been based on a political message, one for which the search for the aforementioned *Angolanidade* took the forefront. The logic of this comes as much from Neto's talent as a writer and thinker as it does from the epoch in which he lived:

> Given the period during which Neto's published poetry was written, broadly speaking 1947 to 1962, it is not surprising that its dominant themes should be those of cultural nationalism; the celebration of those qualities which can make Angolans proud again; the denouncing of the ills which the Africans of Angola have suffered; and, finally, exile and the need to return to a newly created Angola. (38)

Whether or not his political or other leanings held a direct relationship with Pan-Africanism, or simply from the more linguistically-limited wish to see a free Angola / Lusophone Africa, is not necessarily the subject of the present debate[67]. His poeticized reality, in fact, would

---

[66] This influence was not limited to poetry. As seen previously, Luandino Vieira's work also shows a level of inspiration from the Brazilian Modernists.

[67] In returning to Bvuma's poem one may observe an evidently Pan-African application of his image, in a somewhat archetypal manner.

serve as part of the greater cause for national freedom from the Portuguese Empire, not only in his own work but also in the overall approach to writing literature during this period, beyond a single poet's verse (Matta, *Literatura*, 80-81).

The literary, as all other possible cultural manifestations, would then serve the will of the nation (this, of course, would translate into a literature whose primary function would be that of a supportive service to the state; the utopian ideals of the time would not reveal this side of the discourse until later on, nonetheless). This would become an essential element of the revolution against the Portuguese. "… através da experiência de seu povo, se definira e se solidificara sua prática revolucionária, de que a literatura seria um dos instrumentos" (Calvão 2) (" … through the experience of his people, his revolutionary practices would be defined and solidified, from which literature would be one of its instruments"). Among his influences on Angolan literature, the place he engendered for literature in defense of the cause of national identity may have been the most telling of all, well beyond his evident placement within the national revolutionary canon.

In speaking of the external influences on his poetic voice in general terms, and rather ironically, the cause of the Portuguese Neo-Realists seemed to have played an important role in his development as a writer. Their focus on societal woes and the need for greater equality in reference to the strict social hierarchy (reminiscent of a late feudal model, in the case of early 20th Century Portugal) would have caused a palpable reaction in the work of such a politically-inclined author as was Neto:

> [nos] primeiros versos, já se evidencia … o diálogo da poesia agostiniana com as propostas do movimento neo-realista português, fundado sobre o compromisso da denúncia social e da luta por direitos e justiça, o qual, em seu país de origem, revelou-se, sobretudo, com uma consistente reação literária ao autoritarismo do governo salazarista. (Calvão 9)

("[In his] first works, the dialog of Agostinho's poetry with the proposal of the Portuguese Neo-Realist Movement is evidenced ... founded on a compromise toward social denouncement and the struggle for justice and rights, one which, in his country of origin, was revealed, above all, through a consistent literary reaction to the authoritarianism of Salazar's government.")

It seems clear that Neto's poetry founds its roots, at least in part, in the same struggle in Angola (and, to speak in more generalized terms, in the larger part of pre-independence Africa) as that found within the confines of the imperial homeland, Portugal. In this sense, an appropriate understanding of Neto's work and its underpinnings flows out of the common view of an Angolan call to end oppression, entering into dialog with a similar call on the part of the Portuguese themselves. One may then understand his work's defining message in its potential universality, another reason for the extra-linguistic, discourse-based associations presented here. This apparent, internal transnationalism will make the argument for national unity seem even more appealing, an important element to help in leading toward the implicit, parallel poetic argument concerning the Portuguese language in Angola.

Beyond the purely political, one may speak of the metaphorical references which had served as the basis for his poetic realization. There exist images of the people, their daily lives, and the exigencies placed upon them in their struggle to survive under colonial rule, all expected elements of works from this period. As one may also come to expect (serving perhaps as an influence from Neto's own writing on that of future poets and not simply a confluence with his contemporaries), images from nature in reference to the Angolan natural pantheon becomes a powerful symbol in Neto's (and others') verses.[68] The beauty of his southern African homeland will intertwine with a symbolic of struggle as his poetry

---

[68] As Burness has indicated, "[i]n his imagery, ... Neto brings to his poems the people, landscape, trees and animals of different parts of Angola. Life in the musseques is recreated as well as life in the countryside. Those in kinaxixi ..., the women of Lunda, the Bailundos ..., and the Kiocos are brothers in the struggle" (*Fire*, 32).

develops:

> Like many writers of his generation, Neto is sensitive to nature, at once magnificent and the source of immense power. Nature, therefore, provides an inexhaustible supply of metaphors to save the African from his apparent condition of slave. It is as though it was Africa's nature which carried and sustained the traditional virtues of the Africans, virtues which the struggle for independence will redeem. (Chabal, "Aspects," 41)

The link Neto creates between his people, nature, and the power of tradition propel his work into the realm of the mythical. On the same token, and based on the analysis this study intends to show, the same poems will guide the reader toward a pride and self-identity within the nation. That nation, pluralistic and glorious in its diversity (at least in theory), will hinge on various essential and centralizing elements.[69] Language, in its superficially diverse yet simultaneously uniform presentation, will appear as, and remain, one of the core aspects of this new self-identification with the new Angolan nation.

In establishing a basis for the socio-literary analysis of Agostinho Neto's poetry, one must turn to specific examples in order that these elements should be viewed in terms of the principle theme of this study, that is, the poetic expression of concepts surrounding language and that expression's resonance in the creation of an Angolan national identity. This happens within the context of existing interpretations, so as not to lose sight of the richness and potential impact of Neto's poetry. In any case, his collection titled *Sagrada Esperança* will serve as the focal point in reference to his poetry in this vein.

Neto's poetry has been described as the exaltation of suffering as the path to freedom (Matta, "Under the Sign," 55). Throughout the verses of this book, the individual voice becomes lost in the struggle for a break

---

[69] As noted previously and as will become clearer in the next chapter, the contradictions of Neto's discourse will grow explicit as time passes.

from Portuguese colonial rule. "*Sagrada Esperanca* is singularly devoid of poems reflecting the individual and intimate condition of the writer" (Chabal, "Aspects," 38). This focus on the collective good seems to correspond well with the social philosophy to which Neto had ascribed himself. Holness, in his introduction to Neto's collection, reflects on the various themes in the work, darkness (27) and hope (28): "a história épica do alargamento da consciência de um povo lançado num moderno movimento de libertação" (Eng., "the epic story of growth of a people's consciousness hurled into a modern liberation movement") (28). The use of the word "epic" is curiously fitting both with Matta's theory of Angolan poetry's internal epistemological divisions as well as with the contextualization necessary for a work written with the purpose of supporting an anti-colonial revolution. As would be expected, and as will be demonstrated in the examples below, the African natural landscape serves as an "autêntica afirmação da vida" (30) (Eng., "authentic affirmation of life"), in contrast to the life-taking power of the colonizer. This use of the natural pantheon also supports the statements above to that effect, including the desired universal possibilities for interpretation of his verses. Later on this "life" will evolve into the life-giving power of the motherland.[70]

Sagrada Esperança is not divided into subsections; rather, it functions as a poetic narrative of suffering and of the daily battle for livelihood. These central themes will give access to the implicit, yet no less impactful, themes of language use, choice, and preference in the newly forming Angolan nation.

An analysis of a setting-based poem may make clearer the multiplicity of significances which Neto's poetic realization engenders. The poem "Sábado nos musseques" involves not only a poetic description of the "musseques" ("shantytowns," in Angolan Portuguese) but also delves into the cultural practices of the peoples there as reflected linguistically:

---

[70] Such a symbol will find itself transposed into that of the woman / mother which comes to bear, in Tavares' and Kandjimbo's poetic voices, as the essence of Angola itself.

no homem

que consulta o kimbanda

para conservar o emprego

(Neto, *Sagrada*, 42)

...

Ansiedade na kazukuta

dançada à luz do acetileno

ou de candeeiro *Petromax*

em sala pintada de azul

cheia de pó

e do cheiro do suor dos corpos

e de meneios de ancas

e de contactos de sexos

(43)

(Eng.

"in the man

who consults with the curandero

to keep his job

...

Anxiety in the kazucuta[71]

danced to the acetylene light

or to the *Petromax* lamp

in a hall painted blue

full of dust

and the scent of the sweat of bodies

and of hips swinging

and of sexual contact")

The evident focus of the poem centers on various, seemingly unrelated aspects of living in the slums of Luanda. The combined elements of both technologically-enhanced and traditional elements of life there peels back the Salazarist myth of the enlightened (in the sense of Europeanized) and content Portuguese colonial subject. They also emphasize certain carnal aspects of the shantytown dwellers which, if taken without any further analysis, could support the notion of the African colonial subject (and particularly the female subject) as sexual object.[72] Although these verses, pertaining to the same, longer poem, speak of the difficulties of daily life for the typical Angolan, the deeper

---

[71] Kazucuta is a type of rhythmic music found in the area surrounding Luanda proper.

[72] Both of these myths pertain to a Luso-Tropicalist vision of the African colonial subject. This theory, originated in Freire's work on the Portuguese colonies in Africa, is one which Hamilton summarizes in the introduction to his study (*Voices*, 14-16).

level of symbolic discourse present reveals a more subtle yet very important layer to the poem's significance. Here the reader may find both an implied discussion of language as a reminder and reinforcing agent of culture, and the utopic notion of unity in diversity. Remembering Chabal's previously cited comments on language and culture is a very appropriate tool for understanding in this context. From this interpretation, the appearance of the Kimbundu term "kimbanda," or healer, in the context of a culture in pain and in need of healing, reverberates through the second passage cited in which a scene where the spiritual combines with the sexual in what could be a ritual dance superimposed on a moment of suffering.[73] Under this complex framework one may observe that the negative and positive aspects of the described scene (through which the culture is retained and privileged yet also at the point of despair) create a hybridized space. It is this space which supports the notion of nation-building for what Matta's (and the present) theoretical construct(s), on resolving contradictions in the post-colonial condition in Angola and use of language within national unity discourse, each describe.

Beyond concrete poetic moments such as the one above, there exist others which touch upon the more profound sense of what it means to self-identify as Angolan, at least in what the reader will have discovered as the superficially dualistic and outwardly utopian sense which Neto desires to create. The poem "Mussunda Amigo" builds upon the duality of the Angolan identity which Neto means to engender, the Portuguese-speaking one who leads and the non-Portuguese-speaking one whom the first enlightens:

Contigo

Com a firme vitória da tua alegria

---

[73] The healing power of eroticized movement combined with the lack of pleasure in the sexual act, then, counters the stereotype mentioned above. Such an inversion undermines the hegemony of the stereotype, making the image's dual significance that much more complex within an anti-colonial view.

E da tua consciência

O ió kalunga ua mu bangele!

O ió kalunga ua mu bangele-lé-lelé ...

(Neto, *Sagrada*, 79)

(Eng.

"With you

With your happiness's firm victory

And that of your conscience

You whom the god of death has made

You whom the god of death has made has made ... ")[74]

As stated on various occasions in this analysis, Neto's notion of unity in diversity becomes a cornerstone of this identity, linguistically, epistemologically, and in terms of the oppositional confluence of exaltation and pain. The poetic voice rejoices while the Kimbundu one, a citation from a children's song (Hamilton, *Voices*, 85) does not understand but the negative implications (in terms of both unhappiness and over-objectification) of its real context insofar as the environment the poem creates would allow. It should be noted that "Neto writes a very classical Portuguese, not in any sense, like Luandino Vieira, the Portuguese spoken

---

[74] Translation from the Portuguese by the author; translation of the Kimbundu phrases from Russell Hamilton, (*Voices*, 85).

by the people of Angola - even if here and there he introduces words or expressions in Kimbundu" (Chabal, "Aspects," 41). Thus one may conclude that this Portuguese-speaking poetic voice takes the position of knowledge over the other, still in relation of the whole of this identity but with less ability to take more than a politically-correct part in its fruition – an implicit marginalizing of what superficially seems an essential element of the whole.[75] The power of Neto's poetic voice, as with the case of Jacinto's own voice later on, does not depend so much on the nuanced linguistic combinations the reader sees in other poets but on the overall structure which, as Neto becomes the de facto leader of the country in future years, gives him and his government a basis for promoting Portuguese language (intermixed with Kimbundu and other words and phrases) as the primary means of expressing an Angolan national identity. Unity in diversity, then, lives on the surface discourse; national unity of thought, in reality, resides upon an embedded epistemology of Portuguese language as a tool of resistance against the Portuguese colonizers (Severo 31-32) in a rather deconstructive fashion.

In rallying around the hopeful ideal of an Angola identity whose essential parts, when combined, result in both traditional roots and contemporary elements, the oral poetic rite is another area in which Neto's work procures making a markedly profound statement. Examples such as the poem "Caminho do Mato" ("Brush Path") concretize the adherence to this artistic and extra-artistic semantic:

Caminho do mato

caminho da gente

gente cansada

---

[75] This interpretation of the poem takes a less utopian stance than that which Hamilton has expressed in his own reading of the poem (*Voices*, 85). The hope here resides not in contradicting a well-accepted analysis but in augmenting it with our own, appropriately contextualized, post-independence experience of Angolan literature.

óóó-oh

Caminho do mato

caminho da soba

soba grande

    óóó-oh

...

(Neto, *Sagrada*, 46)

(Eng:

"Brush path

people's path

tired people

    ooo-oh

Brush path

Chief's path

Great chief

    ooo-oh")

The various natural elements and images of this poem reside beyond the modern, presenting themselves rather blatantly within the exaltation of the non-urban and traditional ways of life. The poem is clearly a nationalist one, speaking on what one may understand as a pre-colonial and apparently lost piece of the nascent Angolan nation. The reference to the "tired people" in parallel to that of the "Great chief," when interpreted as such, highlights the struggle of the people to continue on their own path, with their own leaders, devoid of outside influence or interference.[76]

It is at this point that it is essential to emphasize the impact of readership of Neto's poems in order to come to grips with the poem's conceivable consequences. Insofar as he would have them presented, the actual target of these poems would have to be the urban populations who would have needed to see them in Portuguese (as well as to those non-urban but very much education readers outside of Luanda or Benguela). It is for these readers for whom his poems may present a window into a supposedly lost way of life (one to which, as far as they may have been concerned, his perspective could return them). Here, in a very direct technique, the poetic voice takes advantage of the oral poetic cadence as an Angolan tradition, transposing the Portuguese language onto it. "His poetry's 'Angolan' quality is not conveyed by a special language but by reference to the history, the people, and especially the natural beauty of Angola" (Chabal, "Aspects," 41). These poetic references, whether performed out of an attempt to codify aspects of the nation which Neto desires to revive, or out of political exigency, play an essential role in re-codifying the Angolan nation, in its diverse facets, in what for all intents and purposes was Neto's own (Portuguese) language.

---

[76] This particular interpretive element becomes more poignant when one considers the political side of the war of independence and the subsequent wars between political party supporters, in which various foreign powers supported their preferred faction with arms, funds, and occasionally troops. Neto, unfortunately, would have been well aware of this occurrence at the time of this poem's composition. This study shall explore the phenomenon in greater detail.

A focus into symbolism from a natural pantheon also appears in other poetic texts by Neto. One such poem would the first of another "collection," called *Poemas de Angola*, taking the title of "Poesia Africana:"[77]

> Lá no horizonte
>
> o fogo
>
> e as silhuetas escuras dos imbondeiros
>
> de braços erguidos.
>
> No ar o cheiro verde das palmeiras queimadas.
>
>
> Poesia africana.
>
> (13)
>
>
> (Eng.
>
> "There on the horizon
>
> fire
>
> and the dark silhouettes of the Baobab
>
> with arms erect.

---

[77] This work repeats many of the poems from *Sagrada Esperança*, so as to make the two seem really as a continuous, circular discourse focusing on the need for nationhood and freedom.

In the air the green smell of the burnt palm trees.")

Despite the sense of hope engendered in the first verse, the second, composed of the words "o fogo," immediately turns both to a violent imagery as well as to a sense of desperation which one may find as sadly fitting with the bellicose context of 1960s Angola. Neto's duplicate use of nature as both adored and destroyed, renewed but ruined, leaves the reader with a simultaneous sense of wonder and of loss, similar to that which the reader of "Sábado nos musseques" would feel, only in this case the poem has the reader focus more on nature (as opposed to a combined natural and non-natural pantheon) in the beginning. (Note 4)

It is in this same vein that one may find Neto's understanding of the nature of the Angolan people in reference to language and identity: his inability to create a true poetic in a language native to Angola, only in Portuguese, both allows his poetic subject to communicate his feelings to the reader, and simultaneously, to alienate himself from many (although evidently not all) of the same people he intends to free (Abdala 121). There is, then, a feeling of supreme national pride on the one hand and, on the other, a certain desolation reminiscent of the poetry of the Brazilian writer Castro Alves, whose work had provably influenced Neto's poetic production (Calvão 14). Authority, within this poetic matrix, will reside in the hands of those who may speak for the rest in what even during the 1960s and early 1970s was fast becoming the common, Angolan language.[78]

Neto's poetic works quickly became part and parcel of his overall political philosophy and the first stages of his eventual rise to leadership in the MPLA and, eventually, to the presidency. The exclusivity of Portuguese language is not the case when viewed through the lens of Neto's poetic idiom; rather, it is the aforementioned utopian discourse of "unity through diversity" which takes center stage. With this in mind, and

---

[78] This self-contradicting recombination is similar to that which Helena Dali mentions in her study (303), although by politicizing this linguistic choice there would arise a loss of trust on the part of the populace.

in viewing this process from a sociopolitical standpoint, this result would, as the MPLA's place became clear during and after the war of independence, locate the Portuguese language as an expression of those individuals at the center of power in the country as well as their supporters. Along with other types of social and (albeit limited) economic movement within the urban and semi-urban sectors, the language attains a level of usefulness not seen in other post-colonial African countries with respect to the implantation of European languages.

Cases exist, however, of poets whose utopian approximations to the Angolan nation's plight would not intentionally lead to a political career; indeed, politics would not be on the mind of Neto's friend and contemporary, António Jacinto (he would serve in the new government temporarily, nonetheless). In Jacinto's example, an unusual one in the overall canon of African literatures although not at all uncommon in the Lusophone canon, the use of the Portuguese language in his poetry expresses his desire to establish a kind of cultural stability during the new nation's fight for independence. It is borne both from his background and of his rather altruistic thematic of harmony through unity.

Born in 1924 in Luanda, Jacinto is yet another example of an African writer whose family is also not of recent African genetic ancestry.[79] The fact of his continual battle against the dominating colonial power is yet even more proof of the true conflict existing in Angola since the 1920s until independence as explained below:

> António Jacinto, em plena infância, começa a ver e a sentir certas contradições entre duas sociedades, a que domina e a outra que obedece. Parece uma luta racial entre brancos e negros, mas não é assim. É uma luta social, durante a qual os dominadores aproveitam para manifestar que se trata de um conflito de luta

---

[79] As Burness has noted, Jacinto's presence within the Angolan literary canon on equal footing as that of a writer such as Agostinho Neto helps to delineate a unique aspect of Angolan, and indeed, Lusophone African literature. He highlights that "...race 'per se' has little or nothing to do with Lusophone African literature" (*Fire*, xiv).

racial. É certo que não podemos tipificar o racismo em Angola tal como se manifesta noutros países de África e tal como se entende na Europa. Neste contexto, António Jacinto procede de uma família portuguesa que se instala em Angola e que não deve ter tido um papel chave no processo colonial. Deve ter sido uma dessas famílias coloniais que não estiveram implicadas com dinheiros, nem com grandes propriedades e não aderiram à política salazarista.

(García 8)

(Eng: «António Jacinto, from his childhood, begins to see and feel certain contradictions between two societies, the one that dominates and the other which obeys. It seems to be a racial battle between blacks and whites, but it is not so. It is a social battle, during which the dominators take advantage [of their social context] to express [the idea] that it is a racial fight. It is true that we cannot typify racism in Angola in the same way in which it manifests in other African countries and in the way in which it is understood in Europe. In this context, António Jacinto descends from a Portuguese family that moves to Angola and would not have taken a key role in the colonial process. [His family] would have been one of those Colonial families not implicated with the rich, nor holding great properties and not adhering to Salazarist politics»).

Jacinto studied also in Portugal, particularly in Coimbra and Lisbon, alongside his friend and colleague Agostinho Neto (Laban 150). He was also incarcerated during the war of independence against Portugal, spending time in the infamous Tarrafal de Santiago Prison in Cape Verde. After his escape upon transfer to Lisbon, he continued to serve in the Angolan government through Neto's term as president, eventually returning to Lisbon where he died in 1991.

The experience of the national struggle and loss of personal liberty during his imprisonment seems to have brought Jacinto even closer to his people, at least in spirit. As obviated in the title of one of his most famed works, the turbulence of this period of incarceration (1961-1972) was the catalyst for his work, *Sobreviver em Tarrafal de Santiago*.[80] As Osundare has aptly summarized, for Jacinto "the personal runs on a two-way traffic with the public; private discovery is a potent form of social revelation" (32).

Jacinto wrote not only poetry but also various prosaic works. These tended to reveal both an adherence to the kind of oral literature (in reference to more intimately recognizable storytelling techniques) toward which Neto would simultaneously turn in his own writing (albeit through the songs and chants imitated, as mentioned earlier), as well as the desire for independence that characterized Angolan literature in the period. An example of Jacinto's such sociopolitical views, stemming from his experience as a former prisoner of the Salazar Regime as well as a citizen of the newly formed Republic of Angola, may be found in his novelette, *Em Kiluanji Do Golungo*[81]:

> A justiça dos homens é curta e incerta, a injustiça larga e amarga. Na verdade, nada há que seja mais caro aos homens e lhes inspire mais respeito que a boa administraçao de uma humana e prudente justiça. Meu filho, sê e procura ser sempre justo, ainda que em teu prejuízo pessoal. A justiça é como leve e amena aragem, em carícia breve, nos dias em que o calor nos importuna. Por má administração dela muito se há sofrido já no mundo. (8-9)

> (Eng: «Man's justice is short and uncertain, a wide and bitter injustice. In truth, there is nothing more valuable to men nor does that inspire more respect from them than the human and

---

[80] I must emphasize that, unlike the case of Neto who spent a relatively short time in prison for his pro-independence activities (Calvão 18-9), Jacinto spent more than a decade imprisoned due to his anti-colonial stance.

[81] The word "Kiluanji" referring to an early colonial-period King of part of what is now Angola, as well as to a town in the province of Golungo Alto, this being a region of Modern Angola.

prudent justice of a good government. My son, be and seek always to be just, despite your own prejudice. Justice is as a light and gentle breeze, a brief caress, on days when we are annoyed from the heat. Many in this world have suffered from poor governance.»)

Here the notion of justice walks hand-in-hand with the ideal of good government that pro-independence literature would reveal indicative of a national, as opposed to a colonial, government.[82] The ideal of the community joining forces against tyranny also plays a vital role in this discourse; the place of the individual should be that of follower or collaborator, not of dictatorial leader. This sentiment could have also stemmed from the oligarchic nature of the Portuguese dictatorship, in which a select few, under the command of Salazar, controlled the whole of the colonial and imperial government; Jacinto, among others, would have been more than aware of this fact.

Here the reader also sees a first person narrative dialectic with the constant presence of motifs from Iberian and local literary traditions. This recombination of themes, symbols, and techniques should not, at this point, seem out of place to readers of Lusophone (whether African, American, or European) literatures. Both here and in other existing analyses of Neto's work such a matrix (as part and parcel of the polysemy that recognizably enriches the literary word) has made itself apparent as a one of the elements representative in forming a cultural hybridity common in Angolan / Luso-African poetics between local practices and existing traditions in Portuguese language in the latter half of the 20th Century.

One may view such a multiplicity of possible meanings in both

---

[82] Although not a primary topic of this study, it should be noted that this notion, when accepted without regard to the social and linguistic strata from which the new governing bodies would be built, would also become an element of paramount importance as the MPLA's hold on power strengthened, to the detriment of the other political parties and other national cultures involved.

Jacinto's poetry and his prose, such as in the example below:

> Meu filho, reclina-te nesse cadeirão, esse de almofadas em que a bordadeira caprichou motivos de Picasso. ... Lá fora, uma lua branca e branda jogará claros e escuros no quieto jardim de suaves aromas melodiosos. ... Então, começarei a contar histórias, ou lidas ou adaptadas (como esta, colhida de Pitigrilli, sei lá quando, algures, em jornal velho), ou vividas e recolhidas de folclore, ou inventadas e rememoradas das que na infância me contou a tua avó ...

(*Fábulas*, 7-8)

(Eng: «My son, sit back in this chair, this pillowed one in which the embroiderer toiled over Picasso-like motifs. ... Out there, a white and blandish moon will throw light and dark in the calm garden of soft, melodic aromas ... Then, I will begin to tell you stories, either read or adapted (as this one, taken from Pitigrilli, who knows when, somewhere, in an old newspaper), or lived and retold from folklore, or made up and memorized from those that your grandmother told me ... »)

The narrative voice describes the story he is about to tell as one read from a European text. As such, the reader may see symbols such as the moon and the breeze as much from a Eurocentric perspective as from that of a more local, "Angolan" one. Yet, the latter view takes hold as the space in which the story takes place is not European; no matter where the text was written, the reader (or participant) in the act of retelling exists in an Angolan spatial framework. It is in this way one may judge that the rewriting of symbolism pertaining principally to the colonizer (namely, the Portuguese) in a newly post-colonial scenario is not an alien notion in literary works of this period. It does not detract from the more local focus of the writer within a political context of a desire for freedom from this colonizer, either.[83]

---

[83] One should find it notable, nonetheless, that a universalized epistemology within a

One should also take note of the self-evidenced fact that the poetry of Jacinto does not dwell in larger philosophical realms of literary inclusion or canonization. In a manner reminiscent of Neto, Jacinto's poetry promotes a vision of cultural hybridity, utopian outcomes of the independence struggle, and the physical reality of the Angolans of the late colonial period as a symptom of the wider ills of Portuguese colonialism. As an example, the inclusion of "crianças de várias cores" (Eng. "children of various colors") in his own work, according to an interview in which he expounded on his literary ideals, (Laban 552) serves as one variant of this idea. Unlike Neto, and most likely due to his own background, Jacinto's poems do not take any particular focus against the colonial subjects of Portuguese descent insofar as they do not oppose his independence-based ideology.[84]

The example below, "Monangamba," serves to illustrate many of the ideas delineated above, including the incorporation of words not found in traditional Portuguese:

Naquela roça grande não tem chuva

é o suor do meu rosto que rega as plantações;

---

relatively localized context does seem to preclude the work's inclusion within the auspices of other post-colonial, African writings from the so-called "Anglophone" and "Francophone" worlds; indeed, the work opens itself up to a re-reading within a wider context by way of such explicit inclusivity. The liminal status of the Portuguese-speaking world within the larger context of the other African literary "worlds," mentioned here and in previous chapters, then becomes obvious when remembering the general literary and artistic criticism on African literatures and literary tendencies. In this respect, and rather ironically, it seems that by reminding oneself of liminality through self-inclusion which serves to marginalize the subject, Sousa Santos' assertion that the Portuguese-speaking world is still considered "semi-peripheral" in this context (*Pela Mão de Alice*, 58) remains intact.

[84] One should note that Hamilton interprets Jacinto's poetry from a racially stratified ideological base, viewing much of his symbolism in regards to black Angolans themselves as equal yet under the rule of whites, or as "two destinies bound to each other, even while one dominates the other" (*Voices*, 87).

Naquela roça grande tem café maduro

e aquele vermelho-cereja

são gotas do meu sangue feitas seiva.

O café vai ser torrado,

Pisado, torturado,

Vai ficar negro, negro da cor do contratado

Negro da cor do contratado!

Perguntam às aves que cantam,

aos regatos de alegre serpentear

e ao vento forte do sertão:

Quem se levanta cedo? quem vai à tonga?

Quem traz pela estrada longa

a tipóia ou o cacho de dendém?

Quem capina e em paga recebe desdém

fubá podre, peixe podre,

panos ruins, cinquenta angolares

"porrada se refilares"?

Quem?

Quem faz o milho crescer

e os laranjais florescer

-- Quem?

Quem dá dinheiro para o patrão comprar

máquinas, carros, senhoras

e cabeças de pretos para os motores?

Quem faz o branco prosperar,

ter barriga grande – ter dinheiro?

-- Quem?

E as aves que cantam,

os regatos de alegre serpentear

e o vento forte do sertão

responderão:

-- "Monangambééé..."

Ah! Deixem-me ao menos subir às palmeiras

Deixem-me beber marufo, marufo

e esquecer diluído nas minhas bebedeiras

-- "Monangambééé..."

  (Apa 65-6)

(Eng.:

There is no rain on that great plantation

it is the sweat from my face that wets the plantations;

There is ripe coffee on that great plantation

and that cherry-red

are drops of my blood turned to sap.

To *A Nação*, with Love

The coffee will be roasted,

trampled, tortured,

It will become black, black like the man under contract

Black like the man under contract!

They ask the birds who sing,

the happily serpentine streams

and the dry plains' strong wind:

Who awakens early? who goes out to the fields?

Who brings the sling

or the bundle of oil palm fruit down the long highway?

Who clears the fields and in payment is disdained

rotten cornmeal, rotten fish,

ruined rags, fifty Angolars[85]

"a beating if you act up"?

---

[85] The «angolar» was a common currency of Angola before independence.

Robert Simon

Who?

Who makes the corn grow

and the oranges blossom

-- Who?

Whose money is it that buys boss's

machines, cars, women

and black men's heads for engines?

Who makes the white man prosper,

be big-bellied – have money?

-- Who?

And the birds who sing,

the happily serpentine streams

and the dry plains' strong wind

will answer:

-- "Monangambééé..."

Oh! Let me at least climb the palms

Let me drink marufo, marufo

and let me forget, diluted in drink

-- "Monangambééé...")

It is possible to divide the poem into two principle sections, the first being the description of life on a coffee plantation, and the second a call to question the subjugation which has led to that life. There is an evident and meaningful use of common words and terms from rural Angolan culture (such as the terms "Monangamba," referring to the coffee plantation worker; "marufo," a liquor made from a native plant but also a term referring to wine; or the phrase "vai à tonga," or going out into the plantations fields), as well as colloquial expressions from Angolan Portuguese. These encapsulate the process of linguistic appropriation as an essential aspect of Lusophone identity building and its expression through a Portuguese language poetic as described in this study. As seen in particular in the case of Neto, the incorporation of other languages (particularly Kimbundu) into Portuguese signals both a rebellion against the colonizer and the poetic expression, and then re-writing, of Angolan identity into one of a nation built on, as has been stated here on more than one occasion, an ideal of unity through diversity.[86] Racial identifiers as evidenced in both particular vocabulary usage as well as in the

---

[86] Popular poetics and ascribing of colonial historicity within an anti-colonial framework such as this enters into the social and racial discourse as expressed in the poem and as

inferiorization and virtual enslavement of the Angolan worker by colonial masters (with terms such as "porrada se refilares" used to highlight the poor treatment of those workers on the part of the Portuguese) and the implied social stratification which had led to such a division also play an essential role in the poem's ultimate message.

It is worthy of repeating that Jacinto spent a substantial amount of time in prison, approximately twelve years, for his anticolonial activities. There are various poems from *Sobreviver em Tarrafal de Santiago* (Eng., *Surviving in Tarrafal de Santiago*)[87] in which symbols found in his previous poetic and prosaic collections (such as those read in the example above) combine with themes of fraternity and liberty to highlight both the entrapment Jacinto felt during his time incarcerated and his intense desire to see the realization an Angola free of the Portuguese. García states that, as a consequence of the experience:

> ...este livro ... [dá] um sentido modernizador e vanguardista à poesia angolana. Visto que neste livro se configuram novas ideias, novas linguagens e um sentido pragmático das coisas tratadas, isso obrigá-nos [sic] a reconhecer que este poemário está filiado num tempo e num espaço que os futuros investigadores da poesia angolana reconhecerão como sendo uma das etapas mais sólidas da poesia em Angola.
>
> (34)
>
> (Eng: «... this book ... [gives] a modernizing and Vanguardist feeling to Angolan poetry. Given that in this book are presented new ideas, new linguistic forms and a pragmatic sense toward those things studied, we are obliged to recognize that this poetic

---

Martinho comments in her chapter on Angolan cultural identity as a hybridized and self-complicating matrix (235).

[87] The site was a notorious Colonial Portuguese prison used to house «enemies of the state» during the Wars of Independence in 1960s and 70s Africa.

collection is affiliated with a time and space that future critics of Angolan poetry will recognize as being one of the most concrete periods of poetry in Angola.»)

The desire for independence in poetic and political terms is evidenced in the work. Yet, the cultural combinations at the level of poetic structure and metaphor between the Portuguese and Angolan voices in his poetry will also become both acute and substantive as the reader moves through the collection. Although one will not see the kind of linguistic diversity in this work as may have happened in the examples from Neto's work, the unified voice whose epistemological base resides in a palpable cultural hybridity will serve to support the revolutionary social philosophy prevalent in the period.[88] It will also reveal the depth of significance which Jacinto, as poet, creates and then expresses an idealistic yet brave new world through verse.

The work is divided into three parts, each signifying a specific period: the first pertains to the poetic subject's time before imprisonment; the second, during imprisonment; and the third, a reflection afterwards. The evolution of various, hybridized metaphors will function around the central notions of the freedom desired on the part of the poetic subject and denied by the ruling colonial forces. These also imply a need for national unity in order to achieve this goal.

From the first section one finds a poetic subject whose task it is to establish an epistemology of place and condition for the reader. As the reader should expect, this time and place are limited only by the walls of the prison in which the poetic subject resides:

Paisagem Concentracionária

---

[88] The previous chapter covers this notion in greater detail.

Esta é a forma imprecisa

fusão do céu e do mar

linha que não se divisa

nos limites da paisagem insular

O Pico do Fogo é um astro

satélite dos olhos meus

suspenso no ar com lastro

de nuvens:

                enovelados algodoais

Gracioso, Malagueta e montes

casas de pedra que os trepam

são fronteiras a limitar

os limites deste sonhar

Poeta – este viver é incerto

sinta-se o homem liberto

só de meditar

No pensar que é vida que se estua

– a ilha continua

    (*Sobreviver*, 21)

(Eng.:

Concentration-Camp Landscape

This is the imprecise form

a fusion of sky and sea

a line that cannot be made out

from the limits of the landscape within

O Pico do Fogo is a star

satellite for mine eyes

suspended with a ballast of clouds

in the air:

    rolled up cotton knits

Gracioso, Malagueta and hills

stone homes that scale them

they are borders that limit

the limits of a day dream like this

Poet – this living is uncertain

know yourself a man who is free

solely by meditating

By thinking it is life that stews

– the island keeps on)

As the poem evidences, the poetic subject laments his incarceration. In his dreams he envisions his prison as serving, in reality, as a root of salvation, in opposition to the physical reality of his entrapment. According to García, the poem represents:

> uma simplificação significativa sobre as razões de ser poeta, ao sugerir e interpretar (criar também) mundos à medida das suas aspirações e, mais ainda, do povo que sofre a opressão. ... o poeta, na automeditação, encontra-se livre na cela: uma espécie de San Juan de la Cruz, salvaguardando a temporalidade, a mentalidade e as finalidades que diferenciam o místico espanhol do revolucionário angolano. Este é o grande paradoxo, o misterioso dilema de um preso que se sente livre pensando no seu país." (35)

(Eng., "...a meaningful simplification on the reason for being a poet, upon suggesting and interpreting –also creating– words in the measure of his aspirations, and even more so, those of the people who suffer oppression. ... the poet, in his meditations, finds himself free in his cell: a sort of Saint John of the Cross, except for the temporality, mentality and finalities which differentiate the Spanish mystic from the Angolan revolutionary. This is the great paradox, the mysterious dilemma of the captive who feels free when thinking of his country.")

Although not the principle focus of this study, one should observe the contradiction of the imprisoned condition and the mystical freedom of the spirit which the poem engenders as one which foments an imaginary of willful and necessary disobedience to the act of imprisonment. Jacinto's poetic subject will fight to maintain his and his nation's freedom internally even though it will make no difference in the external world. Such a struggle in itself signifies a rebellion against the colonial authorities which had placed him there; this rebellion is an intimate one whose extension to the outside world will transform it into an integral piece of the larger battle for freedom.

Beyond this noted paradox and its greater possible ramifications, one may find in the poem a more specified notion of national identity expressed through the imagery, symbolism, and semiotic hybridity. Each of these poetic typographies becomes interlinked throughout the poem. The first image, for example, is one of a blurred divide between Earth and sky – the loss of designated poetic space. Even the stars cannot hold their form for the "rolled up cotton knits" which obscure them. Only the island itself, the symbol of isolation and place of imprisonment, holds firm in this nationless, walled poetic world. As García has pointed out, the poetic subject's true freedom remains in the thought of liberation; within the greater sociopolitical context as well as the historical reasons for his jailing, the poetic subject's struggle turns from an intimate desire for liberation to a more universal longing for freedom. In terms of the mystical resonance onto which García focuses attention (and thus the notion of a semiotic hybridity, as referred to above), one may posit that the natural symbolism of light and dark within an unbreakable space may lead the poetic subject inward, toward an illumination from the evils which threaten him. This would bring Jacinto's voice closer to that of Saint John of the Cross (again, as García emphasizes in the quote cited above) in an epistemological sense, and that much closer to this voice's liberation in an ontological one. This manner of metaphorical link to an Iberian figure whose philosophy stood apart from that of the authorities of his time implies then a recombination of the contemporary and of the historical. (Note 5)

Also in the first section of *Sobreviver* there appear quintessential motifs of the Lusophone poetic world which exist in a continual link between the various forces that in Jacinto's poetry take part in forging a brave new Angolan nation (at least in the metaphorical sense). One of the more salient ones is that of the sea, "o mar," whose present manifestations result in both an affirmation of the historicity present in the hybrid Angolan psyche as well as the re-writing of that historicity toward a new national identity:

Mar

Hoje

me trouxeram ao mar!

Ventava quérolo vento;

Flamívomo sol

lambia de luz à lâmina

vegetal da Ribeira das Pratas.

Me trouxeram a ver o mar?

Qu'é da minha terra e anseio?

Em que longes distantes mergulha

que me secam as raízes?

Mar!

Pus no meu olhar

Da praia ao afro infinito

Uma interrogação.

Me trouxeram ao mar

Hoje.

Que alegria

(Oh! Mar!)

— ainda sei nadar!

(Jacinto 25)

(Eng.:

Sea

Today

they brought me to the sea!

A plaintive wind was blowing;

a flamboyant sun

licked the blade with a vegetal

light from the Ribeira das Pratas.

Did they really bring me to see the sea?

What of my homeland and my longing?

At what far-flung distances does it submerge

that my roots run dry?

Sea!

I placed a question

from the beach to the infinite Africa

in my view.

They brought me to the sea

Today.

What joy

(Oh! Sea!)

— I still know how to swim!)

    Nostalgia of home appears as an element of a more widespread concept in which quite a few Lusophone authors themselves have reveled more or less in various epochs. This would be the rather topical and almost cliché notion of "saudade." Of course, even in mentioning such a sentiment one must take care to avoid the pitfalls of a Luso-Tropicalist vision, or that pertaining to the heavily criticized and controversial ideal of Portuguese colonization as an enlightening force in what is now the Lusophone World (this could include Brazil and East Timor, although when engendered in the 1920s it referred specifically to Portugal's African colonies).[89] Here, nonetheless, this very stereotypical notion reveals itself within a revolutionary setting, one in which the longing is not for Portugal but for the poet's native land of Angola. In this sense one may observe a poetic expression of Neto's ideal of unity in diversity at a conceptual and possibly multi-national level through the re-writing of a well-recognized symbol from Portuguese and general Lusophone literary imagery; the sentiment from the colonizer, in this vein, becomes re-appropriated for use by the colonized in the struggle against the former. The fifth stanza engenders imagery of the sea drying out the poet's roots. Here the reader may see then yet another paradox of the Angolan / Lusophone self as presented in the poem: the notion of home as a place for the poetic subject to find the prosperity and peace he desires becomes negated because of the same sea that could promise it or bring it within reach. Rather than acting as a link to home for the imprisoned poet, or a place of encounter between life and death as one would expect from the Western literary cannon from which the symbol takes its primary significance (at least in the present context), here the sea becomes a barrier to that which gives life to the poetic voice. The symbol then loses the essence of its iconic, Western meaning, taking on a more sinister one. This novel interpretation of Jacinto's poem corresponds well with the notion that the Portuguese, representatives of the West, use their culture as an impediment to the freedom of another culture.[90] On the same token one may observe that the poem ends with a turn from the elegiac calling to land to a more hopeful declaration of movement, that is, the use of the sea as a place in which to "swim," presumably homeward. As seen in the previously studied poem, Jacinto's poetic subject calls forth for its own salvation from incarceration by appropriating metaphors of the colonizer,

---

[89] Hamilton studies this notion and its potential, when taken as part of a budding national identity, for self-destructive thought it may engender in his 1975 book, as noted earlier.

[90] In the reader's awareness of this argument's apparent simplicity, one must remember that the discourse of the period sought out such simplicity in order to create a concept of nation in Angola which, given the country's linguistic and cultural complexities, would not necessarily be possible through the natural development of the region, a notion about which I have commented in the introduction to this study.

re-tasking them within his own idea of Angolan identity, and utilizing them for the cause of liberation.

In reincorporating the notions of rebellion, historicity, and hybrid metaphor into this new, national framework, one may intuit that the poetic subject(s) who speak in these poems reflects (when seen as the voice of an epistemological reconceptualization of the Angolan artistic self) the possibilities, and perhaps even as a desire on the part of Jacinto himself, for the birth of a new, contemporary poetic tradition. This tradition appears to affirm itself as one in which the colonial framework is not simply rejected; rather, it becomes appropriated and re-appropriated until it satisfies the needs of the new culture it expresses. In other words, certain aspects of Lusophone identity identified and studied here are essential and, in the context of the present discourse, make up a fundamental part of the experience of all Portuguese speakers (Simon 150). The language of this new tradition, given its roots in the haute literary culture of Portugal and the reinterpretation of both it and of Angola's contemporary hybrid acculturation matrix through the eyes of a population which has participated in the colonial authority structure, need be expressed in a Portuguese language which remits to this particular, nascent national culture.[91] Within this socio-literary framework the ideals of home and of homeland, then, cannot be borne of the same notion of Pan-Africanism which, although present in poetry from this period (Simon 146-7), seems of greater, if not of primary, importance in the poetic works and literary criticism in the so-called "Anglophone" and "Francophone" African post-colonial cultures.

Such a contention need not preclude the appearance of certain, particular elements of Pan-Africanist discourse, even if it may not seem to appeal to the poet in its entirety. They simply become re-appropriated

---

[91] Here again one may find implied the argument that, although diversity is a theoretical preference for the leaders of Angolan liberation, a single language would be necessary for the country to exist and survive. This language, as seen through the poetry and prose of other writers of the time (in both this and the previous chapter) would have to be Portuguese.

toward a more focused poetic discussion. For example, the notion of "África-mãe" (Eng: "Mother Africa") reveals itself as a motif of the work, although still within the particular, localized epistemology described above:[92]

> "[e]ssa Mãe-África, que os poetas africanos de expressão portuguesa tanto invocam e dimensionam, é talvez o conceito europeu, espalhado nas ex-colónias portuguesas e, quiçá, nas inglesas também. É um atributo bastante corrente nos países celtas e vikings que, para chamar pátria, dizem terra-mãe. Nós, os galegos, referindo-nos à Galiza, dizemos: a nossa Terra. Isto também se usa com frequência nas regiões portuguesas do Minho e de Trás-os-Montes...Por isso, particularmente, pensamos que o tema foi importado por África." (García 41)

> (Eng. "this Mother Africa, which African poets of Portuguese expression so often invoke and aggrandize, is perhaps a European concept, spread through the Portuguese ex-colonies, and perhaps, through the English ones as well. It is a rather common attribute in Celtic and Viking countries that, in calling [a land] homeland, one says motherland. We Galicians, when referring to Galicia, say: our Land. This is also frequently used in the Portuguese regions of the Minho and Trás-os-Montes ... For this reason in particular we believe that the topic was imported to Africa.")

An example is found in the repetition of the word "Mãe" at the end of each verse of "Ah! Se pudésseis aqui ver poesia que não há!" (*Sobreviver*, 36) (Eng., "If you could see here the poetry that is not!"). Given that the Salazar government has renamed the colonies her

---

[92] Even though this notion would seem contradictory, Pan-African *discourse* was prevalent at the time (even though, as well have seen, the deeper meaning of such a discourse tends to be lost in the literary works themselves). It stands to reason that it would have appeared as a moment of rebellion against the "European," rather than as a unifier. In this sense the utopian nature of poetic discourse as studied here would find its overextension and, thus, a point of breakdown when challenged in the post-independence poetic later on.

"Províncias de Além-Mar" ("Overseas Provinces"), it must then be considered that this notion's "Angolan" use of the term "Mãe" in reference to the motherland and its resonance in Portuguese / Luso-Continental political discourse may also signify (beyond the simple idea of a localized and specifically identifiable homeland) a re-appropriation from its Luso-Tropicalist use by the Portuguese (in reference to *Portugal* as the motherland). In this sense the deconstruction of such an epistemology in this particular poetic context functions in parallel with one in which the true national poetic does not exist (and yet, it *must* exist given its birth through the verses of Jacinto's generation). Each of these elements in this poetic vision ultimately serves to counterbalance the other.

From the second section the reader will see an even stronger continuation of the notion of the national *bildungsroman* as applied in the work. The process occurs within the epistemology of the creation of a struggling nation's identity through the appreciation and inclusion of essential literary and social figures within what one would hope could become a new, national literary canon. Such a discourse focuses on the similar nature of poets of a varied thematic in order that such a process may find its consolidation at the level of national literature and literary output. An example of a poem which both praises and sanctifies a fellow writer may be found below; interestingly, this writer, Alda Lara (whose name appears as the poem's title) "eschews the confessional mode" commonly assumed from female writers in most literary traditions (Burness, "Children," 45):

Alda Lara

Irmã companheira

não se frustrou a vida

de breve interrompida

(longe é o dia

Em que dissemos futuro e

«Por tanto que se não disse

com cordas feitas de limos

se amarraram nossas vidas»)

      No mar de pérolas e corais

      A sombra dum cais sem lenços ...

      Quem desfez nosso sonho?

Em dor merencória

recebemos teu testamento

– esse que é de sofrimento

Em mil raios de rútila esperança

Voltarás

(exige em espera nossa saudade)

E surgirás

das fímbrias da memória

ledos segredos

– alma aberta de contentamento –

se, como tu, nos vires

espargir pelo nosso Mundo

tuas flores

de Amor

       Fraterno e Puro.

       (Jacinto 56)

(Eng.:

Sister, companion

she did not waste her life

so quickly interrupted

(far off is the day

when we told our future and

Robert Simon

«For all that was not said

with ropes made from water weeds

are lives were ever moored»)

In the coral and pearl sea

The shadow of a dock without handkerchiefs ...

Who unmade our dream?

In melancholic pain

we received your testament

– that one of suffering

In a thousand rays of sparkling yellowed hope

You will return

(our longing in wait demands it)

And you shall surge forth

from the hidden corners of memory

jubilant secrets

– a soul open to happiness –

if, as you would, you should see us

spill unto the World

your flowers

of Love

Fraternal and Pure.)

The many symbolic references to specific elements of the sea and of nature aid in concretizing the connection between the poetic subject and the natural pantheon, a common one in many poetic traditions including that of the Portuguese. The image of the missing handkerchiefs from the third stanza remits to the notion of the women taking leave of their men as they part for other shores, another common image from seafaring tradition [found even in the easily recognizable Portuguese fado song "Barco Negro" (Eng. "Black Boat")], reveals that the ability to say goodbye to those lost (to the sea, signifying their return to origin, or death) is also gone. Yet, the second half of the poem reveals the hope that, when Alda Lara returns, her presence may bring "Love / Fraternal and Pure" back to her desperate homeland.

Alda Lara's poetry speaks of the "sonho de libertação," focusing on the feminine yet also building on the theme of oppression, particularly on that of the male figure (Matta, *Literatura*, 109). Her poetic subject speaks of her with both reverence and justified hope, both of which are reflected in the words of Jacinto's poetic subject as seen above. Lara herself, of course, serves as an important literary figure for what at the time would have seemed the powerful yet nascent, national literary canon. In essence, not only does the poem use the hybridized imagery observed before to engender a contemporary Angolan sentiment, the new national Angolan identity from which it was borne may now perceive of itself through its new (and utterly established) literary history, with its own now recognizable canonical figures such as Lara.

From the third and final section of the work a poetic of somewhat idealistic projection toward a hopeful (albeit not yet palpable) future takes shape. This step is a sound one when taking into account the process of isolation, re-encounter with the self and the nation, and the discovery of other poetic voices whose desire for freedom from the colonial yoke is equally as strong:

Se Disser

Se disser a noite é um lago

Direi de marés nos teus olhos

Tempestades num gesto vago

de lábios e beijos de afago

Se disser a Lua é a flor

Imolada num mar de escolhos

Direi de febres, do fervor

de lábios em beijos de amor

Se disser amor como prece

É por amor que me apetece

Direi também Saudade e Dor

Nos lábios-limos anoitece

(Jacinto 85)

(Eng.:

If I should say

If I should say the night is a lake

I will speak of tides in your eyes

Storms of a gesture undefined

of lips and caressing kisses

If I should say the moon is a flower

Offered up in a sea of reefs

I will speak of fever and fervor

of lips in kisses of love.

If I should say love as prayer

Is for the love that I desire

I should also say longing and pain

In slime-lips turn to night)

Although hope for the future appears here, solidarity with the poetic object (whose female identity may represent a lover, the homeland, or a bit of both) and loneliness in isolation from "her" become the two most salient aspects of the poetic subject's experience in the poem, at least in the first stanza. The title, "Se Disser," is conjugated in the future subjunctive, a verbal mode and tense used in Portuguese to express a pending yet still incomplete action, presumably to be fulfilled in the future. On the surface the poems looks to be a love poem, one which hinges on the distance between the lovers caused by the poetic subject's imprisonment. Nonetheless, this poem appears as one which closes the collection at hand, implying a more polissemic reflection on the part of the poetic subject. As *Sobreviver* uses political struggle as a focal point around which themes of unity in hybridity, diversity, and longing are hinged, one may then posit that the poetic subject utilizes this particular set of amorous images to organize these themes as seen so far in the work.

On the other hand, within the framework of imprisonment, freedom, and nationhood, the reader cannot simply assume that the poem cannot hold only an intimate meaning. For example, the poem's form seems to indicate it as part of an incomplete project. The poem's partiality and incompleteness function at the structural level – it seems to follow the strophic pattern of a Petrarchan sonnet (4-4-3-3); however, it stops abruptly in the first verse of what would be assumedly the final stanza. This brings up the question as to whether or not the final verse is actually the fourth of the third stanza or not, set apart perhaps because of the sudden shift in symbolism – from a natural pantheon reduced to its smallest and most insignificant elements, to the end of that pantheon's time (in which all turns "to night"). As Jacinto's poetic subject has already established the homeland (Angola) as having a feminine character (one seen before, and which again appears in the more detailed study of such notions as they are borne through the poetic work of Tavares and Kandjimbo), the longing to become one with that character may serve, in its deeper meaning, as that of a return to a home in which the sea no longer signifies entrapment and distance, but solely freedom and the creation of something greater. In this sense, the pain of separation engenders the love of hope. The notion of freedom (in this case, an individual freedom from imprisonment) may function metonymically as the desire for the freedom of a new and adored Angolan nation. In the final analysis such a symbolism may also serve to reinforce the creation of an Angolan identity in the soon-to-be post-colonial context. It is evident, in any case, that a text which could be read as a love poem takes on a vastly different semiotic pattern when placed within the historical and poetic context of the period, as well as of the vastly more profound and multivariate thematic structure of the overall work.

In sum, the themes centered around engendering a sense of Angolan nationalism through Jacinto's poetry represent the beginning of a process of both building a national identity and attempting to reconcile that identity's internal contradictions. This reconciliation happens, almost ironically, by way of a similar application of a utopian vision of unity through diversity, but with a focus on hybridizing various cultures through a single, linguistic medium, as opposed to emphasizing one culture in a linguistically hybridized context (as is the case with Neto), as well as with the implied suggestion toward a national literary canon. A poetic of hope and love conveys a more profound sense of the loss of freedom and the willingness to help in earning that freedom for others. Of course, there is always the question of linguistic singularity – while in the pre-incarceration poetic one sees a similar approximation to language combination and re-appropriation as in that of Agostinho Neto (stemming from Vieira's prosaic work concomitantly), in *Sobreviver* one observes a subsequent re-acculturation process in which the more traditional Portuguese language and linguistic structures observed allow for a view into the appropriation of a Portuguese political and literary discourse of colonization. This happens vis-à-vis the simultaneity of an anti-colonial stance in opposition to the Portuguese themselves. Such a phenomenon also marks a utopian space within the greater Angolan poetic of the time as a moment in which the idea of unity through both contesting the colonizer and combining his and the non-European identifying characteristics in a sort of synchronic harmony (according to this particular poetic discourse) supports the birth of a new form of nationhood. In this new concept the linguistic patterns may or may not seem terribly important; however, the basis for them (as well as for those who had founded them) remains the language of the colonizer.

The power struggles which begin in parallel to this "first phase" of Angolan poetry will ensure, over just two decades, that this nascent dialect, now known as Angolan Portuguese (when accepted simultaneously with the more standardized, European, variant of the language as a manner by which to establish the concrete process of territorial unity), will become one of the tools of both the building of a national identity and the unfortunately marginal position of those populations whose individual characteristics will have seemed so essential to its birth. The poetics of the period have helped to set the stage for a new society, one in which the former colonizer's language is both adopted and resented by the population, a new linguistic home for a people whose new "unity" will bring about an understanding of the "diversity" they may ultimately lose.

As such, following this artistic expression of the ideals of a new country's linguistic (and thus social) basis, the period which in this study has been designated as the "second phase" of Angolan poetry, in reference to notions of nation building and language appropriation, takes center stage. The apparent contradictions and utopian falsehoods of this "first phase" will come under greater scrutiny as the freedom offered by the MPLA during the war of independence turns ever less a reality in the post-independence period; the recognition of both poetry's usefulness in this critical apparatus and the self-contradicting status of the Portuguese language within this new matrix will also become evident.

Chapter IV: *Phase Two – the Struggle for Nation's Self*

So far under discussion have been the artistic (more specifically, poetic) expression of historical and socio-literary processes at work in the development of an Angolan nation-state. The reader may find a certain focus as well on the place of poetry as a key element of that process within the auspices of an epistemology of unity which supersedes the real and measurable cultural multiplicity of the country. I have defined the "first phase" of this process, that of the poetic reflection on the nascent, national discourse through metaphor and national / super-national symbols of freedom, at times also enhanced by a visible bilingualism meant to engender a notion of "unity through diversity," and a uniquely Angolan cultural recombination appearing to undermine the Luso-Tropicalist ideal. Nonetheless, and in order to understand the true nature of that discourse, the second phase of its evolution, or that of a revelation of the inherent contradiction which mark the discourse upon which the first phase of poetry is based, must also be studied at length. This revelation will come by way of a new poetic, one which appears quickly and takes on important aspects of what is known as a postmodern, deconstructive artistic approach.[93] It will also use similar linguistic strategies seen in Neto's and Jacinto's poetries to emphasize the falsehoods of their approximation to linguistic and cultural hybridity in the nascent Angolan state. The importance of the Portuguese language will not diminish in this "second phase" of Angolan poetry's development; rather, in the examples studied here its significance will rapidly shift from one of writing the national epic through re-writing the country's nations to one of re-enacting the ontological struggle for the nation's quickly vanishing pluralistic self.

---

[93] Interestingly, Leite's discussion of poetry from the 1980s, and in particular poetry by women, uses various descriptors which one could ascribe to epistemological deconstruction. This will be the topic of a future study.

The poetry of both Tavares and Kandjimbo reflects on such a variety of themes within the linguistic framework of Portuguese language in Angola. Most curiously, a certain love of the ideal of the Angolan nation will be revealed as a contrastive figure against a backdrop of linguistic and cultural reductionism, both being essential ontological elements embedded within their respective poetic discourses and the wider discourse (as seen previously) in general terms.[94]

One may observe the beginning of a re-construction of identity within the confines of a discourse favoring a single, national language (with a marginal recognition of the other major languages of Angola) through the poetry of Agostinho Neto and, in more cultural than linguistic terms but still just as essential, in that of António Jacinto. In the 1980s and 1990s, leading into the first decade of the 21st Century, such a move is later contextualized within and outside of the Lusophone space in an anti-hegemonic poetic voice. Such a voice may focus on the plight of woman and marginalized peoples in Angola, within the context of the false hopes of a newly-borne nation, such as that found in the verses of Ana Paula Tavares. It may also look at the intimate experience of belonging to a new regional power, also tied by social position and obligation to that government, and yet not entirely convinced of the veracity of its approach, such as that found in the mimetic criticism of Luís Kandjimbo. One would expect a change of this type to happen over the course of several decades (as Leite has argued). In mirroring the brutal switch from pre- to post-independence status and as evidenced in the works of these and other writers mentioned in this study, this literary transformation took many fewer years than that.

This sudden and rapid shift in poetic perspective and expression constitutes what I have called here the "second phase" of Angolan poetry's evolution, coming to light in the post-independence period and

---

[94] It is possible, in some ways, to argue that this process has mirrored a similar history of nation-state building in the rest of Africa (Chabal 33). On the other hand, and as observed previously, the topic of language use is both explicitly and implicitly tied to the process of nation-building in the Lusophone sphere in Africa, and particularly in Angola, in a manner unique to its socio-historical and literary processes.

continuing to develop during and after the Civil War as a counterpoint to the utopian and unifying (and ultimately contradictory-ridden) discourse of the so-called "first phase." (Again, I must emphasize that the notion of identity as expressed through such an epistemology has served the Angolan state building project, not necessarily to the detriment of the Angolan state itself, but certainly to the all-encompassing philosophy to which it had espoused over the two decades previous to independence.)

A thematically-driven discussion of Tavares's work will open the door to a comprehension of the general theme of disenchantment and linguistic plurality present, in contrast to the rather idealistic image created in the works of poets producing work in the 1950s, 60s, and 70s. Kandjimbo's work, both in augmenting what Tavares' poetry has achieved in terms of questioning discourse and to show a differing trajectory from hers, will illustrate through poetry some of the ways in which the poetic may reflect upon the tensions this process (both epistemological and sociopolitical) may have caused.

In sum, the themes centered on engendering a sense of Angolan nationalism through both Neto's and Jacinto's poetries represent the beginning of a process of building a national identity. I will now approach these, both within the works of individual writers and as a portion of a larger process, one focused on the attempt to reconcile that identity's internal conflicts and complexities through the nation-building process's continued development in both Tavares's and Kandjimbo's poetic work.

Ana Paula Tavares has become the most recognized and representative voices of contemporary Angolan poetry of the late 20th and early 21st Centuries. Her career has spanned over thirty years, encompassing both an academic (in terms of her studies in variety of humanistic and scientific areas) and poetic trajectories. She is, essentially, one of the few writers who has achieved status as both a critic and poet. As she has stated, "I am an Angolan poet, but I'm also a historian, and as such, sometimes everything about me gets all mixed up, to echo Camões, it's a case of the lover transforming into the beloved, and utter confusion ensues..." (Ribeiro 147).[95] Of her published works in all areas of expertise over the past three decades, seven books of poetry may be found.

Tavares's verses tend to center around the themes of female empowerment in the post-independence and (later on) the post-civil-war contexts. Her work encompasses a very individual perspective, one in which the sensorial takes center stage in the metaphorical interpretation of both external events and intimate reactions to them. It is said that "...se desdobra a partir de dentro, numa percepção interior que capta o mundo através dos sentidos: a visão, o olfato, o ouvido, o gosto e o tacto" (Victorino 224) (Eng., "she unfurls from within, in an interior gaze that captures the world through the senses: sight, smell, hearing, taste, and touch"). (Note 6) Her work has been described as a poetic space where "the detail and the concise verse are allied to erotic tension and suggestion" (Leite 161).[96]

One may also observe that her work reflects a dissonance which has become palpable in Angolan culture in both a singular (as in individual) and more universal (or country-wide) sense. Although until the beginning of the 1980s there flourished, as seen in a previous chapter, a period of utopian feeling among poets as borne out from the independence period (Bezerra 49-50), poets such as Tavares become part of a counter-movement which spread very rapidly and during which "...trata-se de um mecanismo de descentramento que procura colocar em evidência o que permanecia nas margens, propiciando a emergência de modos alternativos e diferenciados de se ver e ler o mundo" (50) (Eng, "one may speak of a decentralizing mechanism which seeks to make evident that which had remained in the margins, propagating the emergence of alternate and differentiated modes of seeing and reading the

---

[95] It is of interest to note that, during the interview, Tavares makes mention of Luís Kandjimbo as one of the poets whose work exemplifies that the attainment of some freedom and "autonomy" during the disappointing post-independence period (in both social and literary terms) was a possibility (Ribeiro 149).

[96] As seen here, nonetheless, Tavares' poetic legacy and ontological, artistic framework does not limit itself only to an intimate and relatively apolitical posture.

world"). This movement, of course, rapidly became the dominant viewpoint in both poetry and prose as this study has shown.

Tavares's poetry illustrates a discourse of sexuality and gender which breaks from the former understanding of the poetic text as a solely a function of the nation-building process (52), insofar as the present context is concerned. From this breaking point one may see that both "European" and "African" literary cultures thrive in her work. Nonetheless, these also form a precarious union leading the reader toward a more nuanced understanding of the forces at work in the Angola of the 1980s and 90s. "Põe em cena o desencanto, as desilusões e as incertezas causadas pela guerra civil e pela miséria em Angola ... " (Secco, "Mãos," 392) (Eng., "She places onto the scene the disenchantment, disappointment, and uncertainties caused by the Civil War and by the misery in Angola...").

Within the primary focus of this study, and as one will come to expect from the perspective outlined here, Tavares' use of the Portuguese language is also nuanced in both tone and vocabulary as a result of the epistemological reflection on the cultures which make up contemporary Angola in her verses (Padilha 311). Essays by Tavares such as her 1992 "Países Africanos, Língua Portuguesa, Passado, Presente e Futuro" (Eng. "African Countries, Portuguese Language, Past, Present, and Future") highlight the controversial and historically marked, yet uncontested, situation of the Portuguese language in Africa as "património" (Eng., "Patrimony"), contamination, and the simultaneous "enriquecimentos e emprecimentos das culturas na sua permeabilidade à delicadeza dos processos" (Eng. "enrichment and impoverishment of cultures in their permeability to the delicacy of [linguistic transculturation] processes") (Tavares, *O Sangue*, 44-5).[97] It is from this point of historical and metaphoric dissonance that one may see the conflict generated in the

---

[97] In the same volume, Tavares speaks of the "várias línguas portuguesas" (Eng., "various Portuguese languages") which have developed in different regions, for different social, political, etc., functions or purposes, many of which do not have the best intentions of the people in mind (47).

external ambience of 1980s and 90s Angola as also one intimately linked to that of a violent relationship between the male and female, language and the erotic (Matta, *Literatura*, 119-120), colonial and post-colonial, and "o sagrado" (Secco, "Mãos," 396). One may also observe that, in reference to language hybridity and usage within the power structures of contemporary Angola, Tavares' use of the Portuguese language as both root of her expression and object of consternation evidences the language's place in that society's current evolutionary moment. This is, not only for the purposes of this study but also as a defining element of the general Angolan poetic, an essential part of her poetic discourse and that of other poets of this phase.

Although there are several themes which previous studies of Tavares's work have observed, for the purposes of this study I will make a concerted effort to focus my argument on the notion of language as both a point of reflection for the on-going process of building national identity, as well as in its wider range of possible criticisms to that identity. In such a way one may begin to see the true formation of this "second phase" of Angolan poetry, insofar as I have presented here. The examples below from two of Tavares's better-known works will serve, in a descriptive although not entirely anthological way, to illustrate this point while not losing sight of the previously studied major themes of her poetic realization.

Dizes-me coisas amargas como os frutos (2001), a collection whose first evident thematic focuses on the desperation of a people torn asunder through the horrors of war, forms the core of Tavares's post-conflict poetic expression.[98] Moments such as "Um homem arrancou o seu próprio coração / p'ra fundar a noite / encontrar o caminho / descobrir a voz / construir a fala…" (Eng: "A man ripped out his own heard / to found the night / to find his path / to discover his voice / to construct his speech…") in "Rosto da muralha" (Eng., "Face of the Wall") are telling of both the political and linguistic / expressive facets of the

---

[98] The title of the work reflects the presence of the natural world in Tavares's poems, a fact on which she has commented as far back as 1991 (Laban 850).

aftermath of this violent step in the evolution of the nation-building period in Angola. This particular poem's strategy may seem of interest as it mirrors appositionally the style of discourse used in Neto's verses to express the freedom which speech entails for the individual in rebellion. As one delves further into the work's underlying significance, such polissemic moments of symbolic and metaphorical realization within the denaturalized discourse of what has been denominated here as Angolan poetry's "first phase" will become even clearer.

One of the first poems of the collection may aid in reflecting on both this grand thematic, as well as on the notions of language and nationality. It is aptly titled "Origens" ("Origins"):

Guardo a memória do tempo

em que éramos vatwa,

os dos frutos silvestres.

Guardo a memória de um tempo

sem tempo

antes da guerra,

    das colheitas

e das cerimónias.

Amada

vestiste os passos de chuva

para assistir ao meu fim.

Vens com os mesmos passos

das noites antigas

quando, vestida para o amor,

me preparavas o tempo

com os óleos sagrados da espera.

Amada

tens os olhos vermelhos

do sal e da culpa.

Os celeiros estão vazios

As crianças sem leite.

    (10-11)

(Eng:

I keep the memory of the time

when we were Vatwa,

those of the wild fruits.

I keep the memory of a time

without time

before the war,

the harvests

and the ceremonies.

Lover,

you put on bands of rain

to attend my ending.

You come with the same steps

of ancient evenings

when, dressed for love,

you prepared time for me

with the sacred oils of waiting.

Lover,

your eyes are red

from salt and guilt.

The barns are empty

The children are without milk.)

  Before entering into the detailed analysis of the poem, it should be mentioned that the Vatwa is a small tribe living in the borderlands of Angola and Namibia. They must use various trees and wild fruits as part of their diet, hence the references to both the people and their nutritional practices in the second and third verses of the poem respectively.

There is an obvious geographic displacement of the poetic subject, from the urban center of Luanda (or perhaps her native city of Lubango, in Huíla) to the southern borders with Namibia. It nurtures a story of origin held within the poem, and allows the reader a temporal and genealogical continuity while breaking with the expected spatial one. From here one may begin to observe that the poetic subject is speaking with the "amada," or lover, a female poetic object. The poem, divided into two stanzas and utilizing an easily read and more colloquial vocabulary, gives first the seemingly utopian sense of existence in simplicity and timelessness. This type of discourse reminds the reader of the hope engendered in the "first phase" of Angolan poetry.

The second stanza, nonetheless, brings the reader back to a reality through which there is none of the imagined sustenance, and in which the lover has made promises which s/he has not kept. The contrast of the "salt" and "milk" in this stanza highlight the opposition between the sweet life lost and the bitterness of reality. As there is the precedent of viewing the nation as a female figure in Angolan poetry, and another that views the figure as categorically personified (again, that personification occurs in Neto's and Jacinto's verses and as will appear in the analysis of Kandjimbo's work here), one may assume that the "lover" is Angola, at least in a political sense. She, being the tempting yet false side of the country, or the government supposedly representing the people within such an allegorical description, has offered a utopian space yet has simultaneously ruined that utopia, one which the poetic subject once experienced. In terms of linguistic and cultural plurality, the aforementioned reference to the Vatwa is an important one; it sets the base for an identity to which the poetic subject adheres, despite the evident loss of the lifestyle which this identity marker had entailed.[99]

---

[99] Another example of the topic of the utopia broken through language "unity" in the "crónica" titled "Língua da terra" (Eng. "Language of the Land") from Tavares's 2004 collection *A Cabeça de Salomé*. Here a resident leaves his plurilinguistic home, conquers all outside, then returns and imposes a single language on the people. This has the effect that

In this sense, Tavares' work exemplifies both arguments. Her verses comment both directly and indirectly on language as a tool of expression and oppression, while speaking simultaneously to the sociopolitical failings occurring in the current internal conceptualization of post-colonial and contemporary Angola.

Another example is less a linguistic one and more a type of transcultural commentary; given the thematic tendencies of the work, the poem nonetheless has an essential place in this analysis. The presence of traditional beliefs from Eastern and Southern Angola is a very consistent aspect of both urban and rural cultures in the country; musicians such as the well-known singer Waldemar Bastos have even ensured their inclusion in songs such as "Muxima" from his *Pretaluz* (2003) album.[100] In the case of a poem such as "As Viúvas" ("The Widows"), the poetic subject refers to another borderland, that between life and death, between survival and perishing. It is this reinterpretation of the notions of hybridity which Jacinto first presented during the "first phase" of Angolan poetic evolution that here finds an even more nuanced expression:

Devorei a carne do boi do fogo

tudo até ao fim e o coração

No entanto

Kalunga, oh Kalunga,

"[t]oda a gente fala a mesma língua, mas ninguém se entende" (Eng. "Everyone speaks the same language, but no one understands anybody") (113).

[100] It should be noted that Bastos sings in Portuguese using the urban Angolan (Luanda) dialect, representing in yet another artistic and social stage the widespread use of Portuguese, and, to an extent, the homologation of specific aspects of Angolan culture which has become commonplace in artistic work produced in the country vis-à-vis the current, prevailing political discourse.

como estou necessitada

como preciso de sorte.

Aqui a fome é tanta

que as mulheres devoraram a carne dois bois dos homens

e as que eram virgens envelheceram

ninguén cumpriu os preceitos

                        e agora somos viúvas da floresta

                        e temos os sonhos perdidos

...

    (Tavares 34)

(Eng:

I devoured all of the cow's meat from the fire

until the end and its heart

Nonetheless,

Kalunga, oh Kalunga

how I am in need

how I need good luck.

Hunger here is so

Women have devoured all the men's cattle's meat

and the ones who were virgins have aged

no one complied with the orders

      and we are now the forest widows

      and are dreams are now lost

...)

    Of course, the poem speaks of the horrible suffering of the people as they survive in detrimental conditions. The women's aging symbolizes the loss of innocence in such circumstances; whether married or unmarried, all have become the bearers of pain and sadness at nature's death, thereby becoming nature's widows. Death, their country's, their spouses', and their own, as a poetic motif also allows for the integration of a symbolism which transcends national boundaries. This places the notion of living on the edge of non-living into both recognizably Angolan and Western terminology. In speaking of the actual mythological reference, "Kalunga" refers to the "Kalunga Line," a frontier that exists in the belief systems of various peoples of Southern Angola (and the idea of which has spread throughout the country) between the living and the dead. One may find it similar to the image and significance of the river Styx in Ancient Greek beliefs (although the former would be described as a much wider space) (Asante 361).

    In this sense the meaning of the poem, as those from Jacinto's more (as Chabal would state) "social" or (as Matta would have seen) "constructive" poetic, becomes culturally hybridized. (Note 7) In order to understand the reference to Kalunga one must be familiar with Angolan traditional beliefs; it helps if one keeps in mind the comparison with the metaphoric River Styx, as well. It is through such a base duality that the reader may begin to understand one of the complexities of national identity in contemporary Angola as part of a self-deprecating and contradictory ebb and flow between a violent colonial past, a hopeful moment of independence, and a disillusioned post-colonial present. The need to use the Portuguese language (as opposed to Kimbundu, for example) as the only medium of communication in the poem, despite the evident reference to a credence which exists as foreign to that language, heightens the tensions between colonial / post-independence past and post-colonial present, between national mythologies and starkly disillusioned realities surrounding the poetic voice. In an environment in which the Portuguese language has appeared as the primary tool for communication and dissemination of both the ideals of a unified, singular national identity and the realities of a hegemony of power (on the part of the MPLA-led government), such references, while enriching in a sociocultural sense, also challenge (that government's) power as based in notions of unification through cultural and linguistic unilateralism. They do so by highlighting implicitly the weakness of such a structure and the need to emphasize the cultures which existed before it.

An example from an earlier work, *Ritos de Passagem* (1985), titled "Alphabeto," reflects on language as a way to cover up the true suffering of the people in the post-revolutionary context. Here the poetic discourse moves even closer to an outright attack on the contradictions which have endured since before the war of independence had come to its end:

Dactilas-me o corpo

    de A a Z

        e reconstróis

            asas

            sedas

            puro espanto

por debaixo das mãos

> enquanto abertas
>
> aparecem, pequenas
>
> as cicatrizes
>
> (32)

(Eng:

> You type out my body
>
> from A to Z
>
> and you rebuild
>
> wings
>
> silk
>
> pure appalling
>
> underneath hands
>
> while open
>
> they appear, small
>
> her scars)

    As observed previously, it seems that the poetic word in Tavares's verses is meant to "semear Angola" (Padilha 305) with both language that unifies the nation and deconstructs that nation's own reconstitution through violence and oppression. Again, in both linguistic and cultural terms, the epistemology of a bicultural origin becomes paramount in understanding the poet's work. Her language use, similarly to that in the work of poets such as António Jacinto, is nuanced and refined, yet in a break from that poet's unifying tendencies becomes also daring, critical, and deconstructive.

Tavares, in her view, has concluded previously that her own poetry stems from her combined Portuguese and Angolan origins. Her verses are both worldly and Angolan, feminine and genderless, rebellious and patriotic:

> That is the work I try to do: the incorporation of various heritages, and while my outlook on the world is from that land, that space, I am not blind to the rest of the world. I read poetry from around the world, and am open to the experiences of the world. What I try to do is not confuse things, not to confuse registers, and to work with a legacy that fate put at my disposal. (Ribeiro 152)

It is Tavares' love for her country and fear for its well-being, linguistically, politically, culturally, and intimately which propels her work into such a dynamic and fortuitous poetic space. Although the ideal of the nation will not be lost in the analysis of the next and final poet, as will be observed, the overt metalinguistic critical apparatus remains strong, and perhaps even gains force, in Kandjimbo's work.

Luís Kandjimbo, originally from Benguela, has based his academic and professional career on his work as a civil servant and diplomat. He has served as the Angolan Cultural Attaché in the Angolan Embassy of Lisbon as well as professor at the Universidade Metodista de Angola in Luanda. He is better known as a champion of the arts and as a literary and as a cultural studies critic than as a poet, although his poetic voice would place him within the wider Angolan literary canon (as Ana Paula Tavares had mentioned in the interview cited in this chapter).[101] He

---

[101] Various poems of Kandjimbo's also appear in the rather comprehensive 2011 Anthology of Angolan Poetry titled *Entre a Lua, o Caos e o Silêncio: A Flor*.

has undoubtedly built a successful career as part of the MPLA's cultural hegemony and as, in principle, a defender of Angolan national unity.

It should be noted that his poetry and other writings exist with the purpose of further defining Angolan identity in the post-independence and post-civil-war context, both within and outside of the government-approved confines expected given the current political control over artistic work which the Angolan MPLA-held leadership maintains. His verses, however, are neither revolutionary in the sense of being combative, nor based on a representation of the popular voice of an uprising. It is, in fact, his rewriting and reapplication of Angolan cultural practices and linguistic norms to discuss the uniqueness of his country's position in the greater African, Luso-African, Lusophone, and worldly contexts which places him (in both poetry and critical prose) on the forefront of a new Vanguard in the contemporary Angolan literary space.[102] This is one reason for which his verses are so essential to revealing and defining this "second phase" of Angolan poetic evolution. Kandjimbo has essentially attempted to construct an image of a great Angolan nation while simultaneously bringing to bear the issues that nation faces. Through his poetic subject, the central theme of this study, that is, the of power in Angola and its subsequent reflection through language use as expressed through poetry, will make itself more than evident.

Kandjimbo is author of two poetic collections (up to the time of this book's composition), *A Estrada da Secura* and *De Vagares e Vestígios*. The most recent book of the two, *De Vagares e Vestígios*, will be the principle point of focus given the variety of possible themes, images, spatial contexts, and relational matrices on which the reader may place emphasis.

---

[102] It should be noted also that recent studies on Angolan literature reveal its essential sociocultural function as contestation to the various techniques used by the ruling party, the MPLA, to forge a national identity through the eradication of non-Centrist cultures and subcultures in the country (Arenas, *Lusophone*, 172). Kandjimbo's work places him both within this official discourse and somewhat counter to it.

The work is divided into five distinct sections based on spatial, temporal, and thematic considerations. The first four, *De Vagares* ("Of wanderings"), *Vestígios de Lugares* ("Vestiges of Place"), and *Personagens do Lugar* ("Characters of Place"), *Proversões* ("Pro-versions"), may seem to the reader as one longer section comprised of four sub-sections with the similar themes throughout, although in other areas of focus they differ widely. The first serves to establish a trajectory through which the poetic subject attempts to find the path to move forward in the nation-building project. It is in this sense that Kandjimbo parts from the well-viewed journey of identifying and codifying the ideal of Angolan national identity begun by Neto and Jacinto. The second and third sections offer a poetic analysis of the various elements of individual / mythic, national, regional, post-colonial, pan-African, and universal identity as connoted through the first, moving between different times and geographical spaces in order to do so. The fourth swings the reader back toward the Angolan "homeland" (as Jacinto's poetic subject had suggested through his own poetic evolution), bringing to light re-interpretations of *Umbundu* expressions through the contemporary, post-war Angolan lens (and in so doing reviving Neto's desire to impel the populace into the epistemology of "unity through diversity" as previously observed). The fifth and final section, *Quatro Canções à Fidelidade Conjugal* ("Four Songs to Conjugal Fidelity") is actually a series of more intimate poems culminating in a final, "Impossible Praise" ("O Elogio Impossível"), a poetic conclusion to the artistic study of Angolan national identity (in its various complexities) proposed in the work. The collection, in sum, ascribes Kandjimbo's poetic voice as one of a "constructive" poetic (as Matta would have stated), yet meandering between the "intimate" and "social" foci (as encompassing Chabal's perspective). In terms of the overall placement of his work within the confines of this study's framework, his verses fit well within what I have described here as the "second phase" of Angolan poetry's contemporary evolution. (Note 8)

The poems from first section open the reader to the thematic context described above. They do so utilizing a variety of both erudite and common language, in much the same way as Tavares' poetic voice had previously achieved:

To *A Nação*, with Love

A Nudez Arável

A baía indecisa e solitária

Exposta à voraz cidade

Recolhe na nudez do céu

O olhar falaz e luminoso

Dos limites habitados

Com recorrente sentir na meia noite

A solidão decisiva

Ilumina o limite

Da nudez arável nas esquinas

Na cidade recorrente da meia noite

(9)

(Eng:

Arable Nudity

The solitary and indecisive bay

To the voracious city exposed

Collects up the nudeness of the sky

The fallacious and luminous gaze

Of inhabited limits

As a recurring feeling at midnight

Decisive solitude

Lights up the boundary

Of the street corner's arable nudity

In midnight's recurring city)

The first impression of this scene poem is one which the informed reader may repurpose as a pathetic fallacy of sorts – the poetic voice seeks out company in what are apparently empty streets, applying his own emotional state upon the external and inanimate world. This world becomes converted metonymically into an "arable nudity" (hence the title); it transforms into part of a greater, yet barer and less tolerable space. As such, one observes a beginning in solitude, with the individual in his place at the mid-point between what was and what is, what he is meant to be and what he will mean to be. Aesthetic influences from outside of Angola are also evidenced in the poem, similarly to what was found in António Jacinto's poetic works. Unexpectedly, a binary opposition also evidences itself with the mentioning of historical and synchronic, the terrene and the celestial. There is a definite pattern of finding this imagery as a motif in other Lusophone poetic works, and particularly those from Portugal (works from authors such as Sophia de Mello Breyner Andresen and Joaquim Pessoa highlight this), although, as stated above, Jacinto's poetry has also shown such a tendency. One may ultimately posit that the poetic subject, in this example, expresses metaphorically a need for these outside voices while pertaining to a very local context. This ontological condition, one of partial hybridity in a synchronic sense, belies the trajectory of Angolan poetry in both phases (although particularly in the one now under study) as well as that of the poems from the second section of *De Vagares e Vestígios*.

The second section, *Vestígios de Lugares*, contains poems focused on various canonical sites in the Western World. One could argue that Kandjimbo attempts to place the Angolan capital, Luanda, among these, although I will look here as much at the differences between the diachronically placed symbols which, reflected poetically, construct and / or deconstruct the ideals of nationhood and periphery, as at their potential similarities. In any case, the poem "Paris" [the poem following "Lisboa," analyzed in previous scholarship on Kandjimbo's work (Simon 147)] aids in illustrating the results of the notion of intersection (present in the first section of *Devagares e Vestígios*) with the placement of Angolan culture within a post-colonial, yet still very Western, social system:

> Peregrino lugares do inconsútil pano gaulês
>
> Como primeiro escriba da minha geração
>
> No *Café De Flore* e *Aux Deux Magots*
>
> Demando os que brandiram a palavra
>
> Como arco eterno e renovado
>
>
> Em Paris as marcas, os livros habitam
>
> Na cidade do exílio e de uma glória cristã
>
> (26)

(Eng:

I travel as a pilgrim to places from the seamless Gaul cloth

As my generation's first scribe

In the *Café De Flore* and *Aux Deux Magots*

I denounce those who brandished the word

As an eternal and renewed arch

In Paris the hallmarks, the books inhabit

The city of exile and Christian glory)

The reader begins the poem confronted with the same diachronic and synchronic contrasts which defined the work's first section. The reader cannot miss the very plain and purposeful allusions to French cultural history. The rather stereotypical notion of a decadent, European bourgeoisie pervades the first verses, with the mention of Parisian cafes. The reference to the Francophone as a "Gaul" cloth reminds the reader of the bellicose history of living in an ancient Empire's periphery which resides just behind this posh atmosphere; the "seamless" nature of it gives the appearance of purity and perfection in what one may suppose as a vain attempt to mask the violent past on which such a scene's present was build. Understanding such a moment of deconstruction will become crucial for the next step of this poem's interpretation.

There are, as the reader may observe, indirect references to the religious changes in Angola from a non-Christian to a Christian believe system as the poem ends. The final verse, for example, highlights the notion of Paris as a cultural "center." Given the descriptions of the marginalized state of the Lusophone World as seen in previous chapters of this study, Angola hangs implicitly (vis-à-vis the position of the poetic voice relative to its poetic surroundings) in a social, linguistic, and political periphery with respect to other sub-Saharan communities (i.e., the Anglophone and Francophone).[103] The inclusion of the French language acts as a place marker and as a mark of authority in counterpoint to Portuguese (another European, but now also African, language, if one is to follow the discourse presented in both the "first phase" of Angolan poetry as studied here, as well as in other critical contexts also mentioned), classifying their Lusophone linguistic and cultural inheritance as part of the non-central culture's subject to the extra-Portuguese (and thus central) authority. Concomitantly one may see that Kandjimbo's poetic voice views Paris as the "city of exile," or the place to which one flees, in other words, a place of refugees and of those coming from the periphery rather than one of purely "central" identity. This term may surprise the reader, as a city at the global center would not need, in metonymic terms, to run away; rather, it would befit only the place in which one would hide from the center's authority (an idea not implied in the poem). The diachronic perspective which the poetic voice takes and which undermines the notion of cultural hegemony based on historical purity and innocence also plays a central role in the de-centering of the city at this point in the poem. As such, one may surmise that the moment exists in which Paris, symbol of historical and contemporary authority, becomes itself peripheral, or at least unhinged from its central cultural hegemony, in reference to the contemporary Angolan psyche that does not accept (within the present poetic framework) such a misleading discourse. The final verses of the first stanza, in which the poetic voice, having declared itself the "first scribe" of his "generation," denounces "those who brandished the world / as an eternal and renewed arch" while sitting in a typical Parisian cafe also has the effect of reducing the Parisian symbol of literary authority to a mere place in which this new, centered

---

[103] As Sousa Santos states and as discussed previously, Portugal as an imperial power, as well as the Portuguese people living within their own colonies and those subject to the Portuguese imperial government, has historically taken on a "semi-peripheral" state ("Between Prospero," 9), belonging to the center and to the periphery, and thus, to neither.

Angolan subject may now demand against those who would have been seen as an authority in other circumstances.[104]

When taking each poem as representative of their respective sections, one may conclude that a deconstructive effect has taken place in the first two sections of the work. The first, that of the collective nationalism which Neto's poetry attempts to create and which Jacinto's poetry also implies, is replaced through a similar discourse by a more individual and intimate poetic subject. This new voice may also be a national one, but not from a revolutionary perspective. This strategy should seem similar to that which Tavares has employed in her own work, although with the somewhat differing goal within the symbolic of a more sociopolitical poetic commentary. The second, or the dismantling of the existing literary and international hegemony which places the so-called "north" in a clear position of power, makes itself apparent also in the second section, as is the notion that the Angolan may both fit with, and supplant, the non-Angolan as a possible center literary voice. This approximation makes more specific and identifiable Kandjimbo's desire to see what the reader may call Angola's rightful place in the world hegemonic structure. The reader may then bear witness to the establishment of a new type of national identity, one which attempts to take its place within a new world order and which forces the older linguistic hegemony to cede to a new voice in an older, yet suddenly newer, language. This identity has evolved into one expressed, in as natural a way as it is hybridized and strife-ridden, by an African writer in Portuguese language.

At this point it will be necessary to contextualize this seemingly overzealous perspective further. One need also remind oneself that Kandjimbo's role in the Angola of this period is one of recognizing and fomenting the arts and literature as both a writer and a member of the

---

[104] As an aside, this may also serve to counteract the "colonial nostalgia" apparent in 21st Century Angolan prose (Arenas, *Lusophone*, 190) which adds an unfortunate subtlety to the already complex and hybridized post-colonial Angolan identity. It could also be that Kandjimbo's poetic subject makes its comment to that effect in full knowledge of this new sentiment in present-day Angola.

ruling party. He cannot speak out openly against the policy, although he has also shown himself a defender of artistic freedoms. One may then decide to view his poetic voice's approach as one of "riding the line" between the official MPLA-authored discourse (again, based very heavily on Neto's writings) and the complex suppression of social differences within the force of that discourse's unifying purpose. It then becomes evident, both here and in the poems below, that Kandjimbo is both in favor of a nuanced nation building project but also critical of the threat to non-Portuguese speaking cultures within Angola which this project looks to weaken. This dual process also places Kandjimbo's poetic work clearly within the "second phase" of Angolan poetry.

In the third section, titled "Personagens do Lugar" ("Characters of place"), poems such as *"Cikuamanga,* o Corvo" (Eng., *"Cikuamanga,* the Raven") bring mythical characters into what has been established as a nuanced and hybridized Luso-Angolan identity. This ontological recombination will intertwine in some ways with Tavares' (as well as with Luandino Vieira's) work in terms of approach to multiple, culturally pluralistic manifestations of what in the Western mind may be described as a supernatural belief:

> Com presságio sinistro e antigo
>
> Da podridão e dos homens
>
> Em calculados homicídios de noite
>
> Arquejando cúmplice idade
>
>
> Com bico bafejado voa sobre
>
> Pela sinistra condição dos homens e da morte
>
> (Kandjimbo, *De Vagares*, 31)

(Eng:

With an old and sinister omen

Of rotting and men

In planned nightly homicides

Wheezing complicit age

With a breath-heated beak it soars above

By the sinister condition of man and death)

    One may first note a demystification of the natural, mythic poetic object and references to the violence of past and present. Such recognition of nature's importance throughout Angolan poetry's development and concomitant re-ascribing of this avionic element of the natural pantheon as synecdoche in the contemporary, post-civil war context, should not surprise the reader. As a point of focus linguistically, and in reference to present concerns, the use of the Portuguese language, not combined lexically or syntactically with any other Angolan language(s), takes center stage as the semiotic descriptor of the notions above. It is useful to remember that it also may serve as an element which actually distances the more critically aware, Angolan (or other) reader from this mythical figure of the national psyche.

    As seen here as well as in previous research on Kandjimbo's poetry (Simon 150), the application of Bhabha's mimetics of the official, nation-building discourse becomes a tool to undermine the absoluteness of such a discourse. In the mimetic process, a text will mirror what the perspective of the ill-informed on-looker believes should be the nature of a particular subject. The imitation is imperfect and means to illustrate the weakness of such perspective, thereby deconstructing it (Bhabha 211-212).[105] Through a re-reading of the poem above with this notion of a base mimetic critical approach in mind, it certainly seems that the poetic voice may mean to utilize the symbol of the raven as signifier, not within a mythological framework as the people would see it but as the official discourse would have them see it, as the symbolic devourer of humanity. If this is the case, then it does so without removing the poetic subject's sense of national identity; the symbol of the raven then becomes a highly charged one semantically in the present cultural context for (both the MPLA, whom one could describe as the devourer of the marginalized, and) the Angolan people, watching as the national diversity gives way to a forced and utterly false homogeneity.

In the fourth section, "Nudez e Solidão," the reader observes the return of the metaphor of nudity but with the female poetic body as contemplated through the male poetic verse. This body will transform into a poetic discussion on the question of nation (as in past poetic representations, and particularly those seen in this study, Angola is often referred to as a woman), not in an apocryphal fashion but as an historical and epistemological one. (Note 9)

The poem is based on an *Umbundu* proverb, also cited here as it appears connected with the poem below:

Epele li vala omele; umbumba u vala kuteke

(A nudez aflige
pela manhã;

a solidão feminina
é de noite que aflige)

---

[105] For a more enhanced view of the mimetic critical matrix, one may refer to Bhabha's article listed at the end of this study.

A nudez dói pela manhã

Ao anoitecer a mulher sofre a solidão

A solidão da mulher, a nudez da mulher

É de noite

É como a nudez do corpo

(Kandjimbo, *De Vagares*, 37)

(Eng:

> *Epele li vala omele; umbumba u vala kuteke*
>
> (Nakedness afflicts in the morning;
>
> it is at night that feminine solitude afflicts)

Nakedness hurts in the morning

In the evening woman suffers solitude

Woman's solitude, woman's nakedness

Is nightly

It is like the body's nakedness)

The presence of the proverb itself harkens to an exaltation of the oral literature which has distinguished Sub-Saharan African literary and artistic genres in recent times (Batibo 42-43), including the children's songs in Neto's poems (Hamilton, *Voices*, 85). The meaning of the proverb finds expression through its division into two equal parts, the night and the female body. Loneliness afflicts both; however, the body is also born of the night, making a total excision impossible. Thus, the poeticized woman suffers from both a divided self and a united self. Such a contradictory, yet pervasive, experience reflects the general thematic of Kandjimbo's work, that of the Angolan experience as one of both historical intercultural exchange (at times peaceful, at other times horrifically violent) and *intranational* hybridity. There have been several allusions to this national ideal, analyzed from previous poems and referencing the topical philosophy of "unity in diversity" espoused during the independence period, in Neto's and Jacinto's poems. In fact, even the theme of the poem by Knopfli, a Mozambican author cited previously and written in the same period as Neto's *Sagrada Esperança*, harkens to such an inexistent yet desired intercontinental and pluralistic African identity. It is also of note, and as such a point to continue to emphasize, that the female body becomes a representative symbol of the Angolan nation, particularly in pre-independence period poetics but evidenced also in the post-civil-war era. Its presence aids the informed reader in extrapolating the larger sociopolitical significance of the symbol's relevance to the current study (both here and in the analysis of the poem following).[106] This complexity is one from which the Angolan as individual and as part of a larger nation cannot escape, at least according to the argument Kandjimbo's poetic subject seems to make. Yet it has also allowed Angolans a uniquely universal place in a larger pan-African context while maintaining a vital link to the cultures not allied with the MPLA's centrist vision (as also indicated earlier).[107] This transforms, then,

---

[106] For a more detailed study of this phenomenon, please refer to Ana Sofia Ganho's study of representations of femininity in Angolan poetry cited in the Works Cited section.

[107] I will again note here that, concomitant to Jacinto's use of specific terms from Angolan Portuguese in his poetic work, the linguistic combinations noted in African dialects of Portuguese is also a phenomenon which, when combined with influences noted from the linguistic inventiveness of the Brazilian author Guimarães Rosa and as evolved in Luso-African post-colonial prose works of authors such as Ondjaki and Mia Couto (Arenas, *Lusophone*, 163-5), offers readers of the world a fascinating perspective rarely studied

into yet another reminder of how the official discourse is appropriated at the level of the Angolan ruling class yet also reflective of a wider process of acculturation, reflecting on the status of this very nuanced and complex nation building process. (Note 10)

The fifth and final section serves to encapsulate and reflect upon the thematic developed throughout the work, as well as to suggest avenues of thought concerning these. It concludes the work with the poem, "O Elogio Impossível" (Eng., "The Impossible Praise"):

Quando uma mulher frondosa e úbere

De um olhar que voraz

Madura exala perfumes e húmus, num sorriso se diz

Não há louvor ou elogio possível

Ergue-se uma voz quente, sondável

Quente narrada por lábios legíveis

Uma voz branda como a sede de um quarto crescente

Irrompendo pelo corpo pródigo e frugal

Injustamente colhida pela memória dos dias

O sol vergastado por mãos sonolentas

---

outside of Anglophone and Francophone African literatures. It also should be observed that, although not necessarily the purpose of this study, the sociopolitical ramifications of such a hybridized poetic work require special attention, particularly in the context from which Kandjimbo's verses are born.

To *A Nação*, with Love

Ó que mulher frondosa e úbere

Libertando perfumes frescos e húmus, num sorriso voraz

Mas é sol vergastado por mãos sonolentas

Não há louvor ou elogio possível para tanto gasto

    (52)

(Eng:

When an abundant and fecund woman

With a look that voraciously

Matured exhales perfumes and smoke, with a smile that says

There is no praise or possible prayer

A hot, audible voice rises up

Spoken hot by legible lips

A bland voice as the silk of a first-quarter moon

Interrupted by her prodigal and frugal body

Harvested unjustly by days' memories

The sun whipped by sleepy hands

Oh, what an abundant and fecund woman

Loosening light scents and smoke, with a voracious smile

But it is a sun whipped by sleepy hands

There is no praise or possible prayer for such waste)

On the surface the poem seems to speak of a rather sultry and yet very self-tormented female poetic object. An analysis of the metonymic nature of the woman may lead, then, to the more socio-culturally complex and fundamentally more impactful meaning the poem offers.

The symbol of the woman in this concluding poem quickly moves from an attractive to a disturbing figure, replete with repetitive, self-destructive movements meant only to highlight her tortured state. One must now remember that, in many poems previous and in both the proposed "first phase" as well as the "second phase" of Angolan poetry, the female body has represented Angola in a figurative way. In this detailed reading of the poem, and based on this possible metonymic relationship, this female poetic object represents the Angolan people in their struggle to find significance in a contradictory social, political, and (more to the purposes of this study) linguistic framework. Within this context, various symbols must take on sociopolitical meanings (as opposed to the previously commented and more superficial discussion of a particular woman's physical condition). Here the scent of perfume, or the discourse of the ideal state whose essential elements one has observed earlier, cannot mask the wasting away and veritable whipping of the nation's body by "sleepy hands," or the laziness of those who would enact the torture. It may then be note that, when placed in comparison to the poetry of Tavares, a poem such as this one reveals both an explicit motif (in the use of the female body to symbolize the self and the nation, both linked as a single entity), as well as a thematic confluence of elements from within the same spatial and temporal limits (such as that of the dissonance between promise and reality felt in Tavares's work). The reader may, as such, proceed to reinterpret the woman's physical state as revealing of the greater, national affliction which has becomes both that of undesired application of an unrealistic ideal and of self-enacted torment. The poetic subject recognizes that, in a situation of repression and simplification of the self's inherent complexities, that self (here representing the nation) resorts to self-flagellation and the wasting of opportunities to recuperate a lost way of being. When viewed from the lens of poetic expression of contemporary Angolan's linguistic uniqueness, the reader may see that the same process has occurred in Tavares' poems as well as in Kandjimbo's verses from earlier in the collection. That is, one may realize that, like cultural suppression, linguistic unity has brought with it a growing inability to protect and nourish languages and cultures not supported by the Portuguese-speaking, more urbanized regime. One may re-naturalize the Portuguese language, within this artistic context, as the one which the government and much of the population have appropriated (out of preference in the case of the former; mostly out of necessity in the case of the latter), and whose place in the country has become of primary importance due to the increasing push to have the population conform to it (and, in speaking less metonymically, from the pressures of the MPLA-led government). It has the effect of serving to appropriate the cultures who must now speak it, to one degree or another, and in the process forcing them to lose much of their core identities. As Kandjimbo's poetic voice has attempted to reconcile this ontological reformatting, this voice reveals also the detrimental consequences of such loss and, simultaneously, the constructed notion of hegemony and authority which the regime has engendered.

In analyzing language choice and use as part of an overall poetic expression and reflection on Angolan society, I must also note that Kandjimbo's poetic tone may seem rather dissimilar to that of many of his contemporaries. While other writers (as noted in comments throughout this study) have brought various themes to fruition by means of using a very colloquial voice in their writings (José Luandino Vieira, Agostinho Neto, and João Melo come to mind in particular), Kandjimbo's poetic voice, both subtle and poignant, takes the opposite approach to the postcolonial discourse in his poetry. His work reads as very much in tune with the stricter formalities of the language; this includes a marked and deliberately aimed use of other languages as non-conforming yet still aligned poetically with Portuguese (which is not the case in works by his colleagues, many of whom will intersperse Kimbundu or other languages into their Portuguese rather than citing these separately). It is at this point that the very official and formal nature of the poetic voice's written Portuguese becomes clear – the daily conversation between life / death, myth and reality, plays out in a language which is both appropriated and appropriating, in which the (conceptually proposed) Angolan self can both identify with this language and also see it as a tool of continued oppression.

Here, then, one will find in Kandjimbo's verses the reminiscent voice from within the former colonizer, that of Fernando Pessoa's seminal poetic work *Mensagem*, in which the poetic voice takes on a nationalist tone in order to illustrate a related notion – that of the imagined nation of the future, "o quinto império" (Eng., "the Fifth Empire"), which exists as more of a dream than a reality. In fact, much of what has been observed in poetry from the last sixty years yields knowledge of a strain of poetic thought which appeared in Angola during the period that views first the present, then the lost past, in a nostalgically utopian manner similar to that of Neto and Jacinto's nationalist poetic voices toward the future (Matta, "Under the Sign," 55). In a postcolonial and 21st Century context, however, the same mimetic process outlined in a previous study on Kandjimbo (Simon 149-150) are simultaneously applied to his own government's discourse of unity through centrality which is found criticized as well in post-colonial prose fiction (Arenas, *Lusophone*, 172). As part of the government-based project but also implicitly critical of that project, Kandjimbo reaches a certain type of poetic "diplomacy" through which the critical lens may exist without putting the poet into a compromising position within the nation building project.

In essence, the poetic expression of Angolan cultural and ontological hybridity[108] leads to the further conclusion that the nation building project of the Angolan elite utilizes the now widely appropriated Portuguese language as a part of a larger discourse of national unity in an effort to stabilize the populace and protect its own legitimacy. This has allowed the increasing spread of the language into Angolan society at almost all social levels. Again, and in a literary sense, it functions both within the national discourse and against this discourse's utopian thematic / dystopian realities.[109] In this more contemporary, "second phase," of Angolan poetry the mimetic of an official discourse supersedes the actual discourse within the poetic context, as is found also in Angolan prose of the period. This most recent phase serves in fostering an intra- and inter-textual dialog as rich as the cultural and linguistic challenges the peoples of Angola will continue to face.

---

[108] Given the relatively static nature of these elements within this representational poetic space, I have chosen to avoid the term "transnational" to indicate an ebb and flow of identities within such a context. This point will come up for further study in future scholarship.

[109] This is rather unlike the absolute marginalizing of the poorer classes linguistically which happens in other (Anglo- or Francophone) African countries due to the use of English or French (respectively) by the governing classes. As the reader focuses specifically on poetics, the evolution from a combined pan-Africanism, unity through a marginally accepted diversity, and national struggle (in Neto and Jacinto) toward a conflicted yet necessary universality based in the hybrid condition of those pertaining to the new Angolan nation (in the works of Tavares and Kandjimbo) also makes itself visible.

Conclusions

This book has presented an alternative perspective on Angolan poetry's evolution, or perhaps better stated, (r)evolution, from a discourse of utopian dreams to the cry of the country's dystopian realities. It has done so vis-à-vis the use of the Portuguese language for poetic expression, and centered on a study of four poets, each with an essential part to play in the rapid changes between two distinctive poetic phases whose respective frameworks I have outlined and studied at some length.

It began with a study of the way in which the languages of Sub-Saharan Africa have found themselves in conflict with those of the former colonizers from Britain, France, and Portugal, focusing first on the methods by which the first two had attempted to unify their colonies under a single, all-encompassing language (English, French, or Portuguese, respectively). This attempt has, of course, failed in the post-colonial era, not due to a lack of interest on the part of any single African national government, but due to a mismanagement of the educational and other bureaucratic institutions charged with such a task. The arts have also played a vital role in expressing metaphorically, in various modes and utilizing a variety of genres, this and other cultural processes in the region.

The study then moved its focus toward the Lusophone, or Portuguese-speaking, African countries, with a particular focus on the two largest, Angola and Mozambique. From a diachronic perspective, as well as a comparative one, the chapter dedicated to this topic has outlined the major features of language change in 20th Century Lusophone Africa. The differences, mainly those related to the joint governmental, religious, and private-sector influences on the spread of Portuguese, have illuminated the principle causes for the relatively higher number of native or near-native Portuguese-language speakers in these countries when put up against their so-called "Anglophone" and "Francophone" neighbors (with the exception of South Africa, for reasons outside of the purview of this study). In this sense I have suggested that, in line with analyses of the issue, language policy cannot be implemented without some sort of historical sense of linguistic bond between the populace and various important non-governmental institutions. The sociopolitical lens widened to include a summary of how the poetic interacts to foster, foment dissent, and / or criticize various aspects of these developing societies.

The chapter following moved its view more specifically toward Angola, although never truly leaving behind the notions of pan-Africanism or of the general "Lusophone" perspectives presented previously. The study outlined the various existing theoretical frameworks and interpretive structures presented over the past two decades to describe the different tendencies and trajectories in Angolan poetics and the interpretive, critical voices concerning these. I have focused mainly on the dichotomies presented by Matta and Chabal in their seminal works on Lusophone literatures and Angolan poetry. I have endeavored to show how the theoretical framework I present differs both from these as well as from another, very similar view on which Leite expounds in her essential, critical work. Finally, I have also given illustrative examples, analyzing and then problematizing the existing theories given the topics studied to this point and to suggest a distinctive epistemology for the discussion at hand.

It is here that this book has offered an alternative framework for the understanding of Angolan poetics from a socio-linguistic viewpoint. Here it is possible to see Angolan poetry from the perspective of Portuguese language's use as a tool for the MPLA's national project and in which the linguistic appropriation seen in Angolan society and literatures becomes bimodal (rather than more of a unidirectional relationship as is the case presented in previous scholarship as well as outside of the Lusophone sphere in Africa), evolving in two separate "phases." The so-called "first phase" distinguishes itself through the expression of a discourse of "unity through diversity," encompassing all within a common communicative structure, namely, the Portuguese language as it has developed in Angola (thus engendering what is now recognized as the "Angolan Portuguese" dialects). In this phase the poetic (and prosaic, as revealed in more than one example) serves the needs of nation-building in a process of linguistic appropriation and acceptance insofar as the model both criticizes colonialism and speaks to the liberation of the Angolan people from the yoke of Portuguese colonialism. This phase lasted until shortly after independence, circa 1975. The "second phase," according to the present analysis and in respectful disagreement with previous scholarship on the subject, happened very quickly; by the early 1980s the clear movement against the previous phase's utopian discourse had grown to include almost all writers of the generation. This is not only due to an incorporation of techniques available through the postmodern artistic criticism apparent since before this phase began, but also as a response to the dysfunctional manner in which the Angolan government has managed the already widely spread Portuguese language within a fundamentally reductive and unifying contextual discourse.

As stated previously, four authors were chosen to exemplify these two phases as expressed through this new framework. From the "first phase" I have presented examples from the writings of Agostinho Neto and António Jacinto. These compatriots from the pre-independence student movements in Angola and Portugal both wrote with national liberation in mind. However, while the former focused on the daily struggles of Angolans and reflected on diversity as part and parcel of the push to create a single, Angolan national identity, the latter chose to place the cultural exchange between colonized and colonizer on the forefront of his poetic subject's discursive trajectory.

Two poets who exemplified the "second phase" were Ana Paula Tavares and Luís Kandjimbo. Tavares's poetry, while already well known as critical of the treatment of women and minority groups in Angola, would reveal a tendency toward pluralism and a desire to see a return to the promises made during the revolution which the subsequent regime had broken under the new light of the framework presented in this study. Kandjimbo concomitantly restated this ideal in a way similar to that by which both Neto reflected on the need for diversity vis-à-vis a pluralized voice and Jacinto reaffirmed the need to contextualize Angolan identity within and outside of the new nation's borders. Each writer very much criticized the government's false dedication to the dream of "unity in diversity," yet each has shown, in dialog with previous poetic / artistic trajectories, a love of nation which transcends the discourse and extends into an almost idealistic notion of hope for the young country's future in these regards.

In terms some logical and sensible conclusions that one may reach based on the study presented here, there exist several. First, I have endeavored to expound on the argument that the modern place of the Portuguese language in Angola is not limited to recent socio-political phenomena. It is one built on centuries of slowly expanding contact between Portuguese traders, missionaries, and other entities, reiterated and redefined through events and rapid social changes beginning in the 1950s and continuing to today. The language took on various aspects of neighboring languages but did not evolve further than to the point of forming a distinctive dialect of Portuguese. Such a process only reinforces the language's place in Angola, as set apart from that of other African countries whose official language is a European one (yet where the total number of measurably native speakers is, for the most part, fewer than 10%).[110] It even placed the country in a separate classification from those territories in which the Portuguese language evolved, through constant contact with the languages of peoples forced to residency there, into a creole (the languages spoken in Cape Verde and São Tomé e Príncipe serve as apt examples, although in these countries Portuguese is an official language spoken by the majority of the population concomitantly with "creole"). This underlies the almost total marginalization of European languages, outside of official channels, in much of sub-Saharan Africa; it also distinguished Angola within a majority of the Lusophone African sphere. When set against the relative acceptance of Portuguese by the majority in Angola (and to a lesser extent Mozambique and Cape Verde, naming the latter with the caveat of its bilingual majority) the procedural issues of implementing a non-native language become clear. In any case,

[110] Here, again, I have excluded South Africa, as the populations of speakers of Afrikaans, English, and various other languages belies the existence of a larger majority of European descent. This is not at all the case in Angola (or the rest of Lusophone Africa), although the presence of literary figures of European genetic ancestry has been noted on several occasions in this study.

and in order that this process may happen in favor of the former colonizer's language, the pre-colonial languages (and as such, the cultures using them) would come under pressure to conform to this now national, Angolan language. The current regime in Angola has placed much emphasis on this while also producing a discourse of "unity in diversity" when referring to the now relatively marginalized cultures of the country. Having stated that, the Portuguese language in Angola finds itself in a contradictory state of having become necessary for the socio-literary expression of an Angolan nation and detrimental to the continued multiplicity of voices which that nation's own discourse of independence and uniqueness continues to represent. Certain contemporary social processes and the passing of each generation, when accompanied by the literary production of Angola happening more and more exclusively in Portuguese, accentuate the problem further. This is not only an Angolan problem; it is a uniquely Lusophone one which has not passed with the leaving of the Portuguese Army in 1974 and one which will pervade critical discussions for a long time to come.

In speaking solely of the critical theories explicated and studied over the course of the present discussion, it is apparent that, while certainly not out of date, the pre-existing theories on Angolan literary development and classifications of periods or trajectories, when taking language use from a mere supposition to an intentional element of the discourse, requires recontextualization. It is precisely this re-evaluation of the critical perspective on the connection between the linguistic, the political, and the literary that the present study has attempted to reconsider and consolidate. By including the diachronic processes of language and politics, as well as an overall context of sub-Saharan and / or specifically Lusophone African 20th Century pre- and post-independence histories, I have questioned the notions that literature may simply have bifurcated within a single directional evolution. Rather, I have posited that it has followed a more temporally-based path, seeking resolution to the perceived issues of non-conformity on the one hand, and a need for respectful governance on the other. Language use, a visibly more complex process here than in most other countries in the region, has not only served the purposes of transforming the country from a top-down standpoint but has also taken on a dual role as appropriated and appropriator. In this sense the Portuguese language, through literature, has revealed its own bilateral function in Angola, to the detriment of the push on the part of the MPLA for the people's total surrender to it (one for which, as the adage goes, actions have spoken louder than words). I also argue, and with good cause, that the literary had begun as an absconded and very prescriptive method of control, turning quickly into a descriptive and implicitly rebellious method of contestation. It is this switch from the so-called "first phase" of the new Angolan poetic (detailing a relatively prescriptive view of the Angolan national identity) to the "second phase" (in which the critical and deconstructive apparatus has been turned against this discourse while maintaining an open conversation with it) which becomes the study's principle focal point.

As a final conclusion, I have turned my attention to the specific metaphorical uses of specific symbols throughout contemporary Angolan poetry and poetics. The first of these, or the natural pantheon, has served to illustrate both the beauty and fragility of the land which the Angolan people have fought to defend, first from the Portuguese, and then from each other. The reader has seen that, while the poets of the "first phase" had extended the symbols from nature into a utopian discourse of liberation, the poets of the "second phase" deconstructed the semiotics of the previous phase's presentation in order to highlight the destructive force which such a discourse represents. Here it becomes evident that the same beauty sought out before independence is ruined afterward by those who had spoken in its defense to begin with.

This process of creation and unfortunate revelation underscores other symbols and references between the two phases. That of the woman, as a symbol of the nation, unleashes the critical eye of Tavares and Kandjimbo while in the same breath these poets show their sympathies toward her. The sea, so gently contradictory in Jacinto's work, is overturned in that of later poets whose transcontinental view wreaks havoc on the simplistic bi-culturality of this poet's sense of both self-proclaimed symbol of "Angolaneidade" and self-constructed otherness –

in short, as the various parts simultaneously of an embattled, ontological semi-whole.

In this vein, then, the study enters into the issues of otherness within and outside of the Lusophone space. Ultimately the question of the peripheral must find some sort of answer; the adoption of the Portuguese language in Angola and the resulting ramifications of such a process in her social, literary, and political realms must respond to it. If such a linguistic and cultural appropriation continues to dwell in what Sousa Santos has described as the "Calibanized Prospero," then such a model on the part of the MPLA, although again based on a longer term historical process, could actually backfire. Nonetheless, it is this complex and perpetual problematizing of the Lusophone identity to which contemporary Angolans belong (whether by choice or by force) that continues to shape and define the national psyche and the nation's / nations' place within the larger regional and world contexts. Only time will answer this enigma and aid the Angolan people in finding their place within themselves, their region, and the wider Lusophone and extra-Lusophone world. Here, then, the love of nation and the search for self intertwine to build upon decades and centuries of cultural evolution and revolution, bringing about the daily redefinition of what it means to be Angolan.

As a final note, and in pondering the various conclusions to which one may arrive regarding the topic(s) of a book such as this one, I find myself, as does the informed reader, before a series of related and unanswered issues which at some point will need to find resolution. These reside in the areas of the literary, the extra-national, and the creation of new modes and genres in the 21st Century.

Although the aforementioned critical frameworks which have aided in classifying and explaining Angolan poetry's thematic and epistemological tendencies, as the reader's understanding of these theoretical constructs' limitations becomes better defined, the field of Lusophone Studies will need to create a greater and more flexible critical apparatus to encompass that which it as a whole does not comfortably describe. For example, there may be a need for further study on the reuniting of the intimate ("constructive") poetic and the "epic" (nation building) poetic, as Matta has indicated, from the thematically-driven interpretive approach, to which Chabal has adhered, in the contemporary Angolan context. Particularly given the present study and its focal points which reside tangentially to those essential to the above-mentioned critical voices' perspectives, it is suggested that work begin on a combined framework which may encompass all of these comfortably. A somewhat similar type of (re)combinatory work is going on currently in the natural and space sciences in attempting to join General Relativity with Quantum Mechanics into a single, paradigmatic discourse; the same could be attempted in the context of Angolan poetics of the period in question.

In the realm of the social and socio-political, the recent immigration of Portuguese citizens to Angola looking for work has broadened yet again the notion of the Lusophone as a bilateral and / or multilateral ontological experience in which the (former) colonizer purposefully leaves the supposed "center" and shifts into a dual identity. In this case, it is one of immigrant and worker on the one hand, and descendent of the colonial master on the other. In the context of the Lusophone sphere this is not a wholly uncommon occurrence; the Portuguese are known for leaving the home country for a better life in Brazil, for example, particularly after independence from the Empire. Nonetheless, the changing relationship between Angola and Portugal (including the aforementioned Angolan investments into Portuguese companies in recent years) may only highlight the need for yet another rewriting of the post-colonial and post-independence notions of national identity, sociolinguistic identifiers, and international relations between the former colonizer and the formerly colonized. Further study of how this new relationship will reform ties between the two countries will be essential.

A final point is centered on one of the most un-centered aspects of 21st Century life – technology. The internet, in its practical non-censurability and plasticity in creating and changing, at will, many modes of expression has had the potential to modify, if not completely overhaul, the overall, currently accepted concept of the literary and its place in the world. One prime example is Kandjimbo's *De Vagares e Vestígios*. It may not be found in any bookstore, for Kandjimbo has not desired to have it controlled in a print setting. Rather, it has been available for free via his website (at least to the date of this book's composition). One may also find many of his articles and other works of non-fiction and fiction there; my own contact with him was through e-mail.

Once more, many poets in Angola as well as in other parts of Lusophone Africa have turned evermore to the rapid response of the realm of social media in order that they may build and keep a substantial readership. An example of a younger writer who has forged ahead in publishing over various on-line media in the Mozambican poet is Amosse Mucavele. His poetry may be found almost exclusively via Facebook and, in somewhat more polished versions, found in the Brazilian electronic literary magazine *Zunái*. One may access any of his or other writers' works via any modern digital device, not simply by laptop or desktop computer. In this sense, Lusophone African poets have begun, in these so far limited cases, to follow the model set forth by their compatriots in the Anglophone and Francophone Worlds in order that their poetry should be disseminated in the most accessible and least expensive way possible. A general culture which may have not had access at one time to literature and the arts now has exactly that.

In this way one may also witness the spread of the Portuguese language as facilitated through technology and the arts throughout all of Lusophone Africa, not only Angola. Previously it had been mentioned that the younger generations in the Lusophone countries have been turning more toward Portuguese as their language of choice; the spread of technology, in a similar fashion to that of private and religious education in previous centuries, has facilitated this extension of the language. Despite its "peripheral" stance worldwide, Portuguese seems to be growing as the primary language of evermore peoples in and outside of Angola. This phenomenon will require much closer study.

Turning back toward the larger theoretical models, when faced with such rapid, brusque, and seemingly unstoppable social and literary processes, one must question the very nature of the apparatus have used to define, classify, and otherwise appropriate from a critical perspective the cultures of Sub-Saharan Africa, and in particular, Lusophone Africa. Perhaps it is time to re-write completely this framework, so that rather than attempting to build a relatively disjointed overall theory one may desire to re-draw the lines of the theoretical map. Such processes have already begun in the American and European contexts, with post-postmodern theory, paradigm shift theory, the notion of the transnational self, and others looking to exercise an influence on the newer perspectives being borne from the apparent epistemological chaos. No matter what one choses to make of the changing literary, social, political, or cultural landscapes of the Lusophone World, in the final analysis, it is the "povo" itself who will have to decide its own fate.

Notes

1. Russell Hamilton's study of pre-independence Angolan literature emphasizes a period within what I will designate as the "first phase" as one in which the notion of a literary canon exists but without a framework to support it (*Voices*, 113-115). In this environment Neto will aid in forming the latter.

2. I have chosen to use the term "phases" here rather than "trajectories" or "movements." This is due to the evolutionary process by which the first will feed into the second, serving as its base *modus operandi* rather than as a simultaneous poetic surge (for which the term "trajectory" would better apply) or contrasting break between the former and the latter (for which the term "movement" would have been more appropriate).

3. From this point onward the reader will notice the use of the term "unity through diversity" in quotation. The choice to do so stems from the conceit that it represents, and will continue to represent, throughout both the "first phase" and "second phase" of Angolan poetry's development (as reflected in this book).

4. I should note that later on the same poem moves to the urban, then to the musical, still with the notions of a union of the forces of loss and love. Thus, even though the chaotic world expressed in the former does not appear in the latter, the spatial shifts present there will still appear in this poem.

5. Such a comparison of a diachronic nature could potentially cause a significant decontextualization (and subsequent desensitizing) of the metaphor; however, given the semiotic similarities between the poets and their respective two poetic subjects in this case, the temporal distance between the two may be removed and, thus, considered apt for the intentions of the more contemporary one.

6. Tavares' work, under Matta's framework, would be viewed as "constructive" for its individualized focus and attempts and reconciling broader social perspectives with her own life experiences.

7. I must emphasize this aspect of critical epistemologies surrounding both Jacinto and other poets at this point in order to obviate one of the goals of this book. This contrast between the "social" and the "constructive," although not diachronic under either Chabal's or Matta's framework, tends to function less descriptively than one would hope when the sociopolitical and sociolinguistic contexts, both of which evolve diachronically, are overlapped onto each respective framework. The situation becomes even more confusing if both frameworks are enacted simultaneously, since each reacts to differing approaches. Such a shift in interpretation makes yet more evident the need to re-examine the general understanding of Angolan poetry's overall development, and thus, emphasize the purpose of the present study.

8. Again, by referring to Chabal and Matta within the sociopolitical and sociolinguistic context, one may observe the need for an alternative, critical system of classification.

9. The various motifs present in contemporary Angolan poetics, borne from concerns about language and culture in a context of non-predetermination and realized through natural and corporeal symbolisms, should indicate a general trajectory of metaphorical development in the genre. This may be of interest for future studies, and in particular, of studies on 21st Century Angolan poetry.

10. Whether this "process of acculturation" is a positive or negative result of the linguistic and cultural unification which has occurred in post-independence (and particularly, post-civil war) Angola I

will not venture to judge. I will note, however, that the recent, apparent push by the Angolan government to create a new space for celebration of cultural diversity (yet entirely in Portuguese language and / or "pan-African" languages) (Silva, par 9) highlights the need for a clearer perspective of this process' objectives.

Appendix

Since beginning this study I have become more aware than ever of the multiplicity of approaches possible when looking at African literatures, both within an epistemology of the purely literary and within a contextualized discourse. The difficulties may seem astounding; yet, as with many newer fields of inquiry, the possibilities of enrichment within the area of literary studies and within a more interdisciplinary context are astounding.

More so than ever it is possible to discuss other perspectives. Many exist, such as those of the Portuguese writers who, as former soldiers, colonists (many of whom classify as "retornados," or the returned ones, from the former colonies, having suffered a palpable level of prejudice upon their return to Portugal), and mere citizen observers lived first-hand the war in the colonies, the "Revolução dos Cravos," and the subsequent, dramatic turns of fortune which define contemporary Portugal. Ribeiro, Ribeiro, and Vecchi's co-authored study on the artistic (both literary and audiovisual) expressions of these experiences reveals the multifaceted nature of these narratives, in their poetic / musical, prosaic, or cinematic forms (13-15). Others become uncovered as time goes on, adding their uniqueness to the greater narrative of Luso-African (and specifically, Angolan) colonial and post-colonial studies.

Finally, and with respect to the plurality of voices which have contributed to the development of the theory of Angolan poetry and to the analysis of the various poets and writers whose work I have shown as the artistic points of convergence for such an approximation presented here, it is vital to continue interpreting and reinterpreting both art and its context. The purpose of such a perpetual state of reading and discussion does not stem from a need to create meaning; rather, it is borne from the everlasting and indelible desire to understand, and reflect upon, the complex nature of Angola, her literature, and her many peoples.

Works Cited

"People." *Background Notes on Countries of the World: Republic of **Angola**.* March 2007. 1-7. Web.

"People." *Background Notes on Countries of the World: Republic of **Senegal**.* March 2008. 1-5. Web.

"Portuguese." *Ethnologue.* «http://www.ethnologue.com/language/por». Accessed February 2014. Web.

Abdala, Jr, Benjamin. "Agostinho Neto." in Rector, Monica (ed. and intro.); Vernon, Richard (ed. and intro.) *African Lusophone Writers*. Detroit, MI: Gale, 2012. 120-25. Print.

Abreu, Carreira de. "A Língua faz a Nação: O Caso de Angola." *Vértice*. 72 (May-June 1996): 99-100. Print.

Afolabi, Omoniyi Olusegun. "Regeneration in Lusophone African Literature: Subversion in the Works of Luís Bernardo Honwana, Manuel Rui, Mia Couto, and Ungulani Ba Ka Khosa." Diss U Wisconsin-Madison, 1997. Print.

Afolabi, Omoniyi Olusegun and Burness, Don. "Introduction." Afolabi, Niyi and Burness, Don, Eds. *Seasons of Harvest: Essays on the Literatures of Lusophone Africa*. Trenton, NJ: Africa World Press, Inc., 2003. Print.

Ahluwalia, Pal. "Out of Africa: post-structuralism's colonial roots." *Postcolonial Studies*. 8.2. (2005): 137-154. Print.

Almeida, Roberto de. "Civility." Roundtable on "In Angola." *Angola: Angola President José Eduardo dos Santos Handbook*. Vol 1.

Washington, DC: International Business Publications, DDD. 64-66. «books.google.com». Accessed 23 January 2015.

Apa, Lívia et al, Eds. *Poesia Africana de Língua Portuguesa: Antologia*. Rio de Janeiro: Editora Nova Aguilar, S.A., 2003. Print.

Arenas, Fernando: *Lusophone Africa: Beyond Independence*. Minneapolis, MN: University of Minnesota Press, 2011. Print.

---. "Manuel Rui." in Rector, Monica (ed. and intro.); Vernon, Richard (ed. and intro.) *African Lusophone Writers*. Detroit, MI: Gale, 2012. 159-64. Print.

Asante, Molefi Kete, Mazama, Ama (Eds.) *Encyclopedia of African Religions*. SAGE Publications: Thousand Oaks, CA, 2008. Print.

Assis Junior, A de. *Dicionário Kimbundu-Português*. Santos: Luanda Argente, 1969. Web. "https://archive.org/details/dicionriokimbu00assiuoft." Accessed 14 March, 2014.

Bamgbose, Ayo. *Language and Exclusion: The Consequences of Language Policies in Africa*. Hamburg: LIT, 2000. Print.

Barbeitos, Arlindo. "A Propósito da Cultura e da sua Diversidade II: Identidade Cultural." 26 May 2014. *Cultura: Jornal Angolano de Artes e Letras*. «http://jornalcultura.sapo.ao/eco-de-angola/a-proposito-da-cultura-e-da-sua-diversidade-ii-identidade-cultural/fotos». Accessed 16 January, 2015.

Bastos, Maria Benedita. "Danse de l'histoire, écritures mobiles: enjeux contemporains dans les littératures de l'Angola et du Mozambique." *Revue de Littérature Comparée*. 340 (Oct-Dec 2011): 454-77. Print.

Bastos, Waldemar. *Pretaluz*. Luaka Bop. 2003.

Batibo, Herman M. *Language Decline and Death in Africa: Causes, Consequences and Challenges*. Clevedon: Multilingual Matters, Ltd, 2005. Print.

Bell, David. "Foucault, Conventions, and New Historicism." in Stephen Barker, Ed. *Signs of Change: Premodern, Modern, Postmodern*. Albany, NY: State U of NY Press, 1996. 297-307. Print.

Bezerra, Kátia da Costa. "Uma voz em tensão na poesia angolana dos anos oitenta." *Estudos Portugueses e Africanos*. 33-34.1-2 (Jan 1999): 49-57. Print.

Bhabha, Homi. "Of Mimicry and Man: the Ambivalence of Colonial Discourse." *Ariel*. 4 (2003): 211-219. Print.

Birmingham, David. "Angola." in *A History of Postcolonial Lusophone Africa*. Patrick Chabal, ed. Indiana UP: Bloomington, IN, 2002. 137-84. Print.

Burness, Donald: "Children in the Poetry and Short Stories of Alda Lara." Afolabi, Niyi and Burness, Don, Eds. *Seasons of Harvest: Essays on the Literatures of Lusophone Africa*. Trenton, NJ: Africa World Press, Inc., 2003. 45-53. Print.

---. *Fire: Six Writers from Angola, Mozambique, and Cape Verde*. Afterword by Manuel Ferreira. Washington, DC: Three Continents Press, 1977. Print.

Calvão, Dalva. "Agostinho Neto: O Lugar da Poesia em Tempo de Luta." *África & Brasil; Letras e Laços*. 2006. 1-21. Print.

Chabal, Patrick. "Part I: Lusophone Africa in Historical and Comparative Perspective." in *A History of Postcolonial Lusophone Africa*. Patrick Chabal, ed. Bloomington, IN: Indiana UP, 2002. 3-136. Print.

---. "Introduction." *The Postcolonial Literature of Lusophone Africa*. Patrick Chabal, ed. Evanston, IL: Northwestern UP, 1996. Print.

---. "Aspects of Angolan Literature: José Luandino Vieira and Agostinho Neto." *African Languages and Cultures*. 8.1 (1995): 19-42. Print.

Chirere, Memory. "Zimbabwe: Poems Tackle Liberation Struggle Up to Economic Empowerment." *AllAfrica.com*. «http://allafrica.com/stories/201208200076.html.» Accessed 22 August, 2012. Web.

Cissé, Mouhamadou. "Francophonie et littérature-monde: Enjeux de l'autoréflexion dans Un rêve d'albatross (Kangni Alemdjrodo) et Verre cassé (Alain Mabanckou)." in Francis, Cécilia W. (ed. and introd.), Viau, Robert (ed. and introd.). *Trajectoires et dérives de la littérature-monde: Poétiques de la relation et du divers dans les espaces francophones*. Amsterdam, Netherlands: Rodopi, 2013. 237-54. Print.

Clavis Prophetarum. *Da situação da língua portuguesa em Angola*. «http://movv.org/2008/09/12/da-situacao-da-lingua-portuguesa-em-angola/.» Visited on 24 April, 2013. Web.

Clegg, John and Afitska, Oksana. "Teaching and Learning in two Languages in African Classrooms." *Comparative Education*. 47.1 (2011): 61-77. Print.

Dali, Helena. "Makulusu, memoria bilingüe; O, la búsqueda de la 'angolanidad' en la obra de José Luandino Vieira." in Elvezio Canonica and Ernst Rudin (Ed.) *Literatura y bilingüismo: homenaje a Pere Ramírez*. (Problemata Literaria 15) Kassel, Germany: Reichenberger, 1993. 287-303. Print.

DiGiacomo, Mark. "Teju Cole's *Twitter* Feed and the Politics of Digital Form." *Modern Language Association Annual Conference*, 11 January, 2014, Chicago, IL.

Diop, Boubacar Boris. "African Languages and Literary Creation." in *African Creative Expressions: Mother Tongues and Other Tongues*. Ed. Akintunde Akinyemi. Beyreuth African Studies 89. Breitinger: Eckersdorf, 2011. 22-36. Print.

Embassy of the Republic of Equatorial Guinea. "Equatorial Guinea to join the Community of Portuguese Language Countries." 24 Febuary, 2014. «http://www.embassyofequatorialguinea.co.uk/equatorial-guinea-to-join-the-community-of-portuguese-language-countries/». Accessed 9 January, 2015.

Ferreira, Carlos e Marques, Irene Guerra, Eds. *Entre a Lua, o Caos e o Silêncio: a Flor. Antologia da Poesia Angolana*. Boaventura Cardoso, Preface. Luanda: Mayamba Editora, 2011. Print.

Ganho, Ana Sofia. "Sex in the Shadow of a Nation: Angola in the Voices of Lupita Feijóo and Paula Tavares." in Hilary Owen and Philip Rothwell, Eds. *Sexual/Textual Empires: Gender and Marginality in Lusophone African Literature*. Bristol, England: U Bristol P, 2004. 155-75. Print.

García, Xosé Lois. *Jacinto: A Luta do Poeta-Guerrilheiro contra a Alienação*. Trad. Maria Luís Ganho (from Galician). Luanda: União dos Escritores Angolanos, 1995. Print.

Gatinois, Claire. "Portugal Indebted to Angola after Economic Reversal of Fortune." *The Guardian*. 3 June 2014. «http://www.theguardian.com/world/2014/jun/03/portugal-economy-bailout-angola-invests». Accessed 4 June 2014. Web.

Gikandi, Simon. "Provincializing English." Editor's Column. *PMLA*. 129.1 (Jan 2014). 7-17. Print.

Gohar, Saddik M. "The dialectics of homeland and identity: reconstructing Africa in the poetry of Langston Hughes and Mohamed Al-Fayturi." *Tydskrif vir Letterkunde.* 45.1 (Autumn 2008): 42. Print.

Hacker, Paulette. "*La vie sur terre*: A Vision of the Millenium in Postcolonial West Africa." *The image of the twentieth century in literature, media, and society: selected papers [from the] 2000 conference [of the] Society for the Interdisciplinary Study of Social Imagery.* Pueblo, CO: U Southern Colorado P, 2000. 371-73. Print.

Halme, R. "Angola: Language Situation." in Keith Brown, ed. *Encyclopedia of Language and Linguistics.* 2nd ed. Elsevier: Atlanta, GA, 2005. 260-63. Print.

Hamilton, Russell. "Posturing with Resolve: Poetry and Revolution in Mozambique and Angola." *Literature and Contemporary Revolutionary Culture.* 1 (1984-85): 158-73. Print.

---. *Voices from an Empire: A History of Afro-Portuguese Literature.* Minneapolis, MN: U Minnesota P, 1975. Print.

Harries, Jim. "The Contribution of the Use of English in Africa to Dependency in Mission and Development." *Exchange.* 41 (2012): 279-94. Print.

Hughes, Heather. "Protest Poetry in Pre-Independence Mozambique and Angola." *English in Africa.* 4.1 (March 1977): 18-31. Print.

Inverno, Liliana. "Português vernáculo do Brasil e português vernáculo de Angola: Restruturação parcial vs. mudança linguística." in Mauro Fernández and Manuel Fernández-Ferreiro, Nancy Vázquez Veiga

(Eds.) *Los criollos de base ibérica. ACBLPE 2003.* Madrid / Frankfurt: Iberoamericana / Verveurt, 2004. 201-214. Print.

Jacinto, António. *Em Kiluanji do Golungo.* 2nd Edition. Luanda: União dos Escritores Angolanos, 1984. Print.

---. *Fábulas de Sanji.* Preface by Lopo do Nascimento. Porto: Edições ASA (União de Escritores Angolanos), 1988. Print.

---. *Sobreviver em Tarrafal de Santiago.* Dedicatory Letter by António Cardoso. Lisboa: Editora Ulisseia, 1985. Print.

---. *Vovô Bartolomeu.* Foreword by Manuel Ferreira. São Paulo: Edições 70, 1979. Print.

Kandjimbo, Luís. "A Dimensão Actual e Histórico-Literária de Agostinho Neto." *Estudos Portugueses e Africanos.* 16 (Jul-Dec 1990): 57-71. Print.

---. *De Vagares a Vestígios.* Luanda : Instituto Nacional das Indústrias Culturais, 2000. Web.

---. *Entrevista Luís Kandjimbo.* Interview 10 May 2012. «http://www.youtube.com/watch?v=suiJ1dPJdaU.» Accessed 23 August 2012. Web.

Kasfir, Sidney Littlefield. "Up Close and Far Away: Renarrating Buganda's Troubled Past." *African Arts.* 45.3 (2012): 56-69. Print.

Laban, Michel. *Angola: Encontro com Escritores.* Vol I and II. Porto: Fundação Eng. António de Almeida, 1991. Print.

Laranjeira, José Pires. "Questões da Formação das Literaturas Africanas de Língua Portuguesa." *Colóquio/Letras (Colóquio).* 110-111 (July-October 1989). 66-73. Print.

Leite, Ana Mafalda. "Angola." Chabal, Patrick (Ed.). *The Postcolonial Literature of Lusophone Africa*. Evanston, IL: Northwestern UP, 1996. 103-164. Print.

Levi, Joseph Abraham. "Portuguese and Other European Missionaries in Africa: a Look at their Linguistic Production and Attitudes (1415-1885)." *Historiographia Linguistica*. 36.2-3 (2009): 363-92. Print.

Liebig, Sueli Meira. "We, too, are Africa: Ideology and Protest in Afro-Brazilian Literature." *The Langston Hughes Review*. 16.1-2 (Fall 1999-Spring 2001): 23-38. Print.

Lionett, Françoise. "Languages, Literatures, Pedagogies: The MLA, Africa, and Diaspora Studies." *Comparative Literature Studies*. 50.2 (2013): 219-227. Print.

Madureira, Luís. "Nation, Identity and Loss of Footing: Mia Couto's *O Outro Pé de Sereia* and the Question of Lusophone Postcolonialism." *Novel: A Forum on Fiction*. 41.2/3 (Spring/Summer 2008): 200-28. Print.

Maldoror, Sarah. "To Make a Film Means to Take a Position." *African Experience of Cinema*. London: British Film Institute, 1996. 45-47. Print.

Marcus, Sharon and Best, Stephen. *Surface Reading: an Introduction*. Columbia UP Academic Commons: New York, NY, 2009. «http://academiccommons.columbia.edu/catalog/ac%3A157279» Accessed 6 January 2015.

Martinho, Ana Maria. "Literatura e Confluências Culturais." in *Percursos de Interculturalidade. Volume III: Matrizes e Configurações*. Lisbon: Alto Comissariado para a Imigração e Minorias Étnicas (ACIME) (Observatório da Imigração), 2008. 225-252. Print.

Matta, Inocência. *Literatura Angolana: silêncios e falas de uma voz inquieta.* Mar Além: Lisboa, 2001. Print.

---. "Under the Sign of a Projective Nostalgia: Agostinho Neto and Angolan Postcolonial Poetry." Trad. Vicky Hartnack. *Research in African Literatures.* 8.1 (Spring 2007): 54-67. Print.

Mendes, José Manuel. "Manuel Rui: Uma Identidade Construída da Resistência à Libertação." *Les Littératures africaines de langue portugaise: à la recherche de l'identité individuelle et nationale; actes du colloque internacional.* 28-29-30 November, 1 December, Paris: Fondation Calouste Gulbenkian, Centre culturel portugais, 1985. 99-105. Print.

Mirabeau, Sone Enongene. "Religious Poetry as a Vehicle for Social Control in Africa: The Case of Bakossi Incantatory Poetry." *Folklore.* 122 (December 2011): 308-26. Print.

Neto, Agostinho. *Poemas de Angola.* Jorge Amado (Intro.) Editora Codecri: Rio de Janeiro, 1976. Print.

---. *Sagrada Esperança.* 3rd Edition. Basil Davidson (Pref.) and Marga Holness (Intro.). Lisbon: Livraria Sá da Costa Editora, 1976. Print.

Nielson, Rex P. "Rui Knopfli." in *Dictionary of Literary Biography.* Vol 367. Gale Publishing: Farmington Hills, MI, 2012. p. 93-97. Print.

Norridge, Zöe. "Sex as Synecdoche: Intimate Languages of Violence in Chimamanda Ngozi *Adichie's Half of a Yellow Sun* and Aminatta Forna's *The Memory of Love.*" *Research in African Literatures.* 43.2 (Summer 2012): 18-39. Print.

Olson, Carl. "The Différance that Makes all the Difference: A Comparison of Derrida and Saikara." *Philosophy East and West.* 61.2 (April 2011): 247-259. Print.

Omotoso, Kole and Dennis, Ferdinand. "The Black Intellectual and the Pan-African Agenda in Languages." *Africa Beyond the Post-Colonial: Political and Sociocultural Identities*. Aldershot, England: Ashgate, 2004. 39-49. Print.

Ornelas, José. "José Luandino Vieira." in Rector, Monica (ed. and intro.); Vernon, Richard (ed. and intro.) *African Lusophone Writers*. Detroit, MI: Gale, 2012. 197-208. Print.

Osundare, Niyi. "António Jacinto, Poet of Consequence." Afolabi, Niyi and Burness, Don, Eds. *Seasons of Harvest: Essays on the Literatures of Lusophone Africa*. Trenton, NJ: Africa World Press, Inc., 2003. 29-43. Print.

Owomoyela, Oyekan. *The African Difference: Discourses on Africanity and the Relativity of Cultures*. New York: Peter Lang, 1996. Print.

Padilha, Laura Cavalcante. "Paula Tavares, e a Semeadura das Palavras." in Maria Teresa Salgado and Maria do Carmo Sepúlveda, Eds. *África e Brasil; letras em laços*. São Caetano do Sul, São Paulo, Brazil: Editora Yendis, 2006. 299-315. Print.

Ramazani, Jahan. "Caliban's modernity: postcolonial poetry in Africa, South Asia and the Caribbean." *Cambridge Companion to Modernist Poetry*. Cork: University College, Cork, 2007. 207-221. Print.

Ribeiro, António Sousa, Ribeiro, Margarita Calafate, Vecchi, Roberto. "The Children of the Colonial War: Post-Memory and Representations." *Plots of War: Modern Narratives of Conflict*. Isabel Capeloa Gil and Adriana Martins, Eds. Berlin: De Gruyter, 2012. 11-23. Print.

Ribeiro, Margarita Calafate. "A Heritage of One's Own: A Conversation with Ana Paula Tavares." *Ellipsis*. 5 (2007): 147-152. «ellipsis5ribeiro-tavares.pdf.» Accessed 15 January, 2014. Web.

Rui, Manuel. *Cinco vezes Onze:Poemas em Novembro*. Lisbon: Edições 70, 1984. Print.

Santos, Boaventura de Sousa. "Between Prospero and Caliban: Colonialism, Postcolonialism, and Inter-Identity." *The Luso-Brazilian Review*. 39.2 (Winter 2002). 9-43. Print.

---. *Pela Mão de Alice: O Social e o Político na Pós-Modernidade*. 6th Ed., 1997. Porto: Edições Afrontamento, 1994. Print.

Secco, Carmen Lúcia Tindó Ribeiro. "Mãos Femininas e Gestos de Poesia." in Inocência Mata and Laura Cavalcante, Ed. *A Mulher em África: Vozes de uma margem sempre presente*. 2007. 391-403. Print.

---. "Postcolonial Poetry in Cabe Verde, Angola, and Mozambique: Some Contemporary Considerations." *Research in African Literature*. 38.1 (2007): 119-33. Print

Severo, Cristine Gorski. "Línguas e discursos: Heterogeneidade linguístico-discursivae poder em Angola." *Veredas - Revista da Associação Internacional de Lusitanistas*. 15 (2011): 19-46. Print

Silva, Roque "Lev'arte com iniciativas pelo Dia de África." *Jornal de Angolan on-line*. 17 May 2014. Accessed 22 May 2014. "http://jornaldeangola.sapo.ao/cultura/levarte_com_iniciativas_pelo_dia_de_africa".

Simon, Robert. "Angolan Poetry in a Post-colonial Context: The Poetry of Luís Kandjimbo as a Case Study." in *African Creative Expressions: Mother Tongues and Other Tongues*. Ed. Akintunde Akinyemi. Beyreuth African Studies 89. Breitinger: Eckersdorf, 2011. 146-151. Print.

Smith, David. "Angola's José Eduardo dos Santos: Africa's Least Known Autocrat." *The Guardian*. 30 August 2012.

«http://www.theguardian.com/world/2012/aug/30/angola-jose-eduardo-dos-santos.» Accessed 16 January, 2014. Web.

Tala, Kashim I. *Orature in Africa*. Saskatchewan: Saskatchewan UP, 1999. Print.

Tavares, Ana Paula Ribeiro. *Ritos de Passagem*. Luanda: Rito-Tipo, 1985. Print.

---. *O Sangue da Buganvília: Crónicas*. Praia-Mindelo: Embaixada de Portugal, Centro Cultural Português, 1998. Print.

---. *Dizes-me coisas amargas como os frutos*. Lisboa: Editorial Caminho, 2001. Print.

---. *A Cabeça de Salomé: Crónicas*. Lisbon: Caminho, 2004. Print.

Udogu, E. Ike. "Africa and the Search for Political Stability in the New Century." Uduku, Ola, and Zack-Williams, Alfred (Eds.) *Africa Beyond the Post-Colonial: Political and Socio-Cultural Identities*. Aldershot, England: Ashgate, 2004. 76-91. Print.

Victorino, Shirlei Campos. "Entre Vozes Silenciadas: O Grito Poético de Paula Tavares." in Jorge, Sílvio Renato e Alves, Ida Maria Ferreira (Org.) *A Palavra Silenciada: Estudos de Literatura Portuguesa e Africana*. Rio de Janeiro: Vício de Leitura, 2001. 221-230. Print.

Argus-*a*

Artes y Humanidades / Arts and Humanities

Los Ángeles – Buenos Aires

2017

www.ingramcontent.com/pod-product-compliance
Lightning Source LLC
Chambersburg PA
CBHW020648220526
45464CB00001B/341